TULLAMORE

6 1 AUG 2022

WITHDRAWN

NO LONGER SLAVES

D1426822

You are no longer a slave but a child, and if a child then also an heir.
(Gal 4:7)

Fr Christy Burke C.S.Sp.

No Longer Slaves
THE MISSION OF FRANCIS LIBERMANN (1802-1852)

the columba press

First published in 2010 by
the columba press
55A Spruce Avenue, Stillorgan Industrial Park,
Blackrock, Co Dublin

Cover by Bill Bolger
Origination by The Columba Press
Printed in Ireland by ColourBooks Ltd, Dublin

ISBN 978 1 85607 717 0

Copyright © 2010, Christy Burke C.S.Sp.

Contents

Introduction

A relatively short experience in Kenya had given me some awareness of the wonderful development of the church in Kenya and Africa in general. The enthusiasm and dynamism of the young churches was a phenomenon I considered worth studying. As a subject for a doctoral dissertation, I chose to explore the significance of Francis Libermann, a convert Jew, founder of a missionary congregation and a prominent figure in the missionary movement of the nineteenth century. The Alphonsian Academy specialises in Moral Theology and generally required research within that discipline. Slavery was the moral issue that led to Libermann's involvement in a missionary enterprise.

Slavery in Libermann's time (1802-1852) was the subject of debates throughout Europe and America. At the time there was general agreement that slavery was unjust. The slave trade and slavery were being outlawed almost everywhere. The effects of the slave trade remained. The question arose as to what ought to be done to address the consequences of such an unjust practice over centuries. This is what Libermann tried to answer. Moral discourse is not confined to determining right and wrong; it should explore what ought to be done. With this in mind I attempted to examine one man's effort to redress the horrors of the slave trade and help the victims of the practice.

Libermann is regarded as having some importance in the area of spirituality. He is seen as of some importance in the French School with Olier and John Eudes. Very little had been written on his contribution to mission thinking despite the fact that the congregation he founded was among the missionary groups that had done so much in bringing the gospel message to Africa. The colonial era was practically at an end. African countries were struggling to find their identity and their rightful place among the nations of the world. Catholic missionaries had made a considerable contribution to bringing about the conditions for independence. That era was near its end. African churches were emerging and were bringing new life to their people. The study of the life and work of an unusual type of pioneering missionary opened up a new vision for the future of Catholic mission apostolate. The dissertation was finished in 1977 and like most such works put on a shelf not to be disturbed.

Limiting myself to the research done in the mid-1970s, twenty years later I wrote *Morality and Mission* (Paulines Publications Africa, 1998). This involved rewriting most of the dissertation and omitting the technicalities that were required in the dissertation. In it I tried to let Libermann speak for himself without much effort to evaluate what he had to offer. The book was soon out of print.

Returning to Ireland in 2002 it became clear that something in the nature of a new missionary movement within the church was needed in Ireland. The pioneers of the great missionary movement of the 19th century might have something to offer. They may still have a contribution to make where evangelisation (or re-evangelisation) is needed.

To explore what we find of value in missionary thinking I have revisited the 1998 book, making some corrections, changes and additions. The moral and pastoral problems in Ireland today are different from those Libermann faced. Still, a major issue then and now is how the church in its structures and pastoral work connects with the real issues of the day. Change and even reform are called for and some reflection on the past might be of help.

The general outline is not meant to be strictly academic. The purpose is to show how one man was able to get involved in a serious social issue and work out a way of bringing about change. His insights bore considerable fruit and this gives them credibility and significance even for the very different circumstances of today.

The largest Province of Libermann's congregation now is Nigeria. The congregation is now established in many African countries. The hope is that this book will help in some small way the followers of Libermann to have some idea of his missionary thinking.[1]

1. Henry J. Koren. *To the Ends of the Earth*, Duquesne University Press. 1983. The congregation Libermann founded was soon dissolved and its members integrated into the Congregation of the Holy Spirit founded in 1703.

Chapter 1 gives a brief account of his life to the age of forty. The final ten years are concerned with his mission and this is the subject for the rest of the book. Chapter 2 surveys the mission field to be attended to – the world of the slaves in their struggle for justice. Chapter 3 outlines some of the factors in Libermann's vocation to mission and his response to the call. How Libermann envisaged the condition of the people who were taken into slavery is treated in Chapter 4. Chapter 5 then goes to the fundamental aim of mission which for Libermann was laying the foundation for a church that would be self-ministering as soon as possible. Chapter 6 sees the needs of the wider community and the variety of ministry required. So the need for, and advantage of, a general system of education is examined. Chapter 7 deals with some issues of social and political significance and how missionaries should approach them. Chapter 8 touches on the topic of culture or 'civilisation' in Libermann's terminology. A new chapter (9) is added as an attempt to connect a missionary methodology of the past to the present conditions in the Irish church.

A lot of work has been done on Libermann since my dissertation was finished in 1977. Paul Coulon, in particular, has made an enormous contribution and his work continues. In the past ten years Duquesne University, Pittsburgh, has continued in the tradition of the late Henry Koren to promote research and publications on Libermann. This is important for the English readership. This present work stays with that of 1977 for the most part.

Sources

Libermann's Writings: Complete Editions

1. *Notes et Documents relatives à la Vie et a l'Oeuvre de Vénérable Francois-Marie-Paul Libermann, Supérieur General de la Congregation du Saint-Esprit et du Saint Coeur de Marie,* ed P. Cabon. (Maison-Mère, 30 rue Lhomond, Paris, Ve, 1929-1941). 13 volumes, 8614 pages.

A further volume was added in 1956 – *Compléments.*

(The references given from these are noted as e.g. (ND. IX, 240) Volume 9, page 240)

2. *Commentaire des Douze Premiers Chapitres de Saint Evangile selon Saint Jean* (1st edition, Ngazobil, Senegambia, 1872, 2nd edition, Maison-Mère, Paris, undated) 709 pages.

Quotations indicated by Comm are from the 2nd edition.

3. *Lettres Spirituelles du Vénérable Libermann* (Procure Générale, 30 rue Lhomond, Paris.) 4 volumes undated, 2552 pages, 528 letters. Quoted as LS. (e.g. LS. II, 48).

4. *Régle Provisoire des Missionnaires de Libermann. Texte et Commentaire,* ed F. Nicolas. (Polycopy edition of 1960). Libermann's Rule for the society and a commentary from notes taken by L. de Lannurien from talks given by Libermann to novices 1844-1846. Quoted as Gloss. (Gloss on the Rule).

5. *Écrits Spirituelles du Vénérable Libermann,* Paris, 1891, 696 pages, (ES. 125)

CHAPTER ONE

Libermann and his Mission

For the purposes of this work three well-defined periods shaped the life of Francis Libermann:

A.   Libermann, the Jew in the ghetto of Saverne, Alsace, Eastern France
B.   Libermann in the seminary milieu
C.   Libermann the Missionary

A. The young Jew of the ghetto

Jacob Libermann, the fifth son of a Jewish Rabbi, was born on 12 April 1802. His father, Lazarus, had married Leah Haller in 1788, a year before the outbreak of the French Revolution. The Libermann family took up residence in Saverne in the Jewish quarter where Lazarus was Rabbi for the local community. For centuries, the Jews throughout Europe had been segregated and confined to live in ghettos. Their fate differed from one country to another, but up to the end of the eighteenth century the ghetto was very much part of the way of life of European Jews. In France, the Jews did not have citizen status. Their social position differed, depending on where they lived and the particular brand of Judaism they professed. The Sephardic Jews, who lived around Bordeaux, were in many ways exceptional. They had acquired some privileges from Henry II in the sixteenth century. They gradually acquired wealth, and because of their wealth further concessions were granted later by Louis XVI. These Jews engaged in banking and business of various kinds, especially importing and exporting. They had become integrated into the socioeconomic life of the country and were to a greater extent part of the whole social fabric. There were constant reminders, however, that they were Jews and as such they were not to be trusted. They differed from the Ashkenazi Jews who were much more isolated within society.

The Jews in Alsace, a region in Eastern France bordering on

the Rhine were Ashkenazi. The Ashkenazi Jews were people of the ghetto. For the most part they were poor. They were not entitled to own property except their houses. They were usually surrounded by hostility and prejudice. The language of the ghetto was Yiddish. The truly faithful Jew was not allowed to learn German or French. To be a Jew was to be of the ghetto, and this was taken for granted. True, the ghetto was imposed from without. The civil authorities required that Jews live isolated from the citizens. Imposed by authority, it was also accepted as the way of life for the faithful Jew. The ghetto helped to sustain Jewish ways and establish a strong Jewish identity. The ghetto was not only a physical reality; it established also a social, religious and political mentality. The inflexible piety of the Jews and their distinctive Judeo-Alsatian language distinguished them from their neighbours, although in many respects they blended into the Alsatian environment. Excluded from the normal commercial life of the country, the Jews developed their own ways of making a living. Such ways did not make them popular with their neighbours. The usury and petty trading necessitated by their conditions of life were regarded as among the most degrading of occupations. Shortly after the Libermann couple began their married life, French society experienced drastic changes. Jews in France did not escape the effects of the Revolution.

In August 1789, the Estates General issued its *Declaration of the Rights of Man and the Citizen*. This made it possible for the Jews to claim citizenship and freedom from the restrictions that were imposed on them. Their ethnic origin and religious beliefs no longer made them foreigners. But the Declaration, of itself, was not enough to bring about true equality. The long history of isolation could not be abolished with a declaration. Prejudices remained, injustices continued. Still, the Declaration did have an effect. The Constitution of September 1790 gave Jews full citizenship. The first-born of the Libermann family, Samson, was born in October 1790 into the new regime.

There was a certain irony in the 'liberty' granted to the Jews. And the irony is well illustrated in the Libermann family. The five sons born to Lazarus and Leah became Christians later – a real heartbreak for the devout Rabbi. It was not only the Libermann family that was thrown into confusion. Ironically, the abolition of the ghetto seemed to herald the death of Judaism as it existed in France. Moving out of the ghetto meant abandoning the Torah, the Talmud and the numerous rites and customs that had survived the persecutions and the injustices of centuries.

The defection from Judaism by the five sons of the Rabbi was not exceptional. It was part of the trend of post-revolutionary France; David Drach (1791-1865) was perhaps the most famous of all. He was an outstanding academic, son-in-law of the Grand-Rabbi of Paris and a key member of the Central Consistorial of Paris. He became a Catholic in 1823. Libermann had contacts with him later at critical stages in his life. At the time when Libermann was in a religious crisis and searching for truth before his conversion to Catholicism, Drach met him in Paris and steered him towards the Catholic faith and the priesthood. When Libermann was in Rome in 1840 Drach was Librarian of Propaganda Fide College and played a major part in introducing him to the Roman authorities and to the pope. Apart from these, Libermann did not have very much contact with Drach who engaged in the apostolate to convert Jews to Christianity. This does not seem to have formed any significant part of Libermann's apostolate. Another Jewish academic, Edersheim, became a priest in the Anglican Communion. Theodore Ratisbonne (1802-1884) was baptised in 1826 and ordained priest in 1830. Liberation and integration had ambivalent results for the Jews.

The defections from Judaism were part of a whole system of social, political and cultural changes. I. Levitatis summarises the position as follows:

> The evolution of central monarchies, the crumbling of the medieval social structure, the harnessing of Jewish leadership in the service of the state, Enlightenment as an inner solvent, early capitalism with its emphasis on individualism, a loss of status of rabbinical courts, these were some of the powerful internal factors that spelled the doom of Jewish autonomy. Many declared that emancipation and autonomy were inherently contradictory, that once the individual Jew is granted equal rights, he can no longer claim group privileges.[1]

---

1. 'Autonomy' in *Encyclopeadia Judaica*, Jerusalem, 1971

When Napoleon came to power in France, moves were made immediately to bring some unity to the divided country. The First Consul made a Concordat with Rome in 1801, and the following year, 1802, Catholic worship was officially re-established. This was the year of the birth of Jacob Libermann. The new world of democracy, liberty, fraternity and equality was being proclaimed amid suffering and bloodshed. With Catholic feelings somehow placated, Napoleon turned his attention to the Jews and to integrating them into the new society. He convoked a Sanhedrin in the hope that Jewish leaders would themselves opt for integration. This Grand Sanhedrin was called for in Paris, in February 1807.

Lazarus Libermann, the Rabbi of Saverne, was designated by the Prefect of Strasbourg to represent his community at this gathering. He was among the small minority who refused to go along with the wishes of Napoleon. He stubbornly refused to comply with the wishes of the majority and vowed to remain steadfast in the old way of life. He could not really understand what was happening in the Sanhedrin, much less in the world around him. He could speak neither French nor German. To abandon the way of life he was accustomed to would be to set sail on a sea without means of knowing where he was going. For centuries, his ancestors had endured and accepted the life of the ghetto; to abandon this would be to betray his ancestors and even his God.

So the Rabbi returned to Saverne, determined to continue being faithful to the tradition that he knew. He was pained and grieved by those who sold out to the dictator. His people were divided, and he was in a minority. This only strengthened his resolve to persevere. The divisions among the Jews strengthened Napoleon's hand. He now issued what became known as the 'Infamous Decree.' This abolished the communal organisation of the ghettos and set up consistories to appoint rabbis. The Jews were now integrated into the state. They were obliged to take family names and to conform to the laws of the land. This was the official position of the Jews. But Rabbi Libermann did not accept this state of things.

Despite the Rabbi's determined stand and his efforts to bring up his children in the old ways, his sons, Samson in 1825,

Henoch in March 1826, Samuel in September 1826, Jacob in December 1826 and David in 1837 became Catholics. His daughter Esther and her family remained faithful to the old traditions. Lazarus' wife died in April 1813. He remarried in June of that year. From this marriage two children, Isaac and Sarah, were born. Both remained in Judaism; Isaac became a Rabbi in the city of Nancy.

The eldest son, Samson, left home for Mayence to study to become a Rabbi in 1815. However, he abandoned the Rabbinical studies and studied medicine. He qualified as a doctor in 1820 and he married in 1821. He and his wife took instructions in the Catholic faith and were secretly received into the church in 1825. The conversion of Samson and his wife became public that year and this constituted a definitive break with his father and brought down on him a father's curse for such a defection.

When Samson was erased from the family list, the Rabbi put all his hopes in Jacob. He would take his father's position. Jacob gave himself completely to his studies of the Torah, the Mischna and the Talmud. Any studies other than biblical ones were strictly forbidden. So, up to the age of 22, Jacob Libermann spent his time preparing to be a Rabbi. All this time he was under the tutelage of his father, a demanding teacher even if he was a loving father. Jacob was not physically strong. He was shy and retiring. He fitted well into the ghetto that officially no longer existed. He was brought up to fear everything non-Jewish. He recounted in later life that he ran away at the sight of a priest and fled in terror at the sight of a Catholic procession. As long as he lived with his family he was completely at home in the kind of life his father knew and advocated. But he moved out of the house and away from the paternal supervision. And with this move came significant changes in his religious outlook and social concerns.

The move to Metz was something of a culture shock. Jacob joined a Talmudic school in Metz with introduction from his father to two teachers there who were known to him. One had been a student of Lazarus and had lived in the Libermann home. The reception this rabbi gave Jacob was so cold and uncaring as to leave a memory of rejection that remained with him throughout his life. The other friend of Lazarus did little to alleviate the affront. Jacob was away from home, and he had entered a cold and impersonal world quite different from the home in Saverne. His natural shyness and the lack of warmth from those who were expected to lead him into the ministry left him isolated and abandoned.

The Jewish community of Metz was divided. Recently, it had experienced a degree of prosperity, but now divisions between the liberals, who were anxious to be more thoroughly integrated into the modern society, and the conservatives, who wished to remain with the past and opposed the modern trend, contrasted sharply with the uniformity of the ghetto. Fidelity to his father's wishes would have obliged him to ally himself with the conservatives. But this group did not provide the welcome nor the warmth that was needed in his new environment.

The shift to a more liberal way of living and thinking began with the study of French. The coldness of his would-be teachers turned to hostility. In his French studies he got help from a Catholic and not only help but a degree of friendship that he treasured throughout his life. How much influence this had on his future is hard to assess. It enabled him to form a positive opinion about some Catholics that contrasted with what he was brought up to believe.

Rousseau would not be the kind of reading recommended for a trainee rabbi. Jacob, like many of his contemporaries, delved into Rousseau. *La Profession de Foi du Vicaire Savoyard* had quite an influence on him. Another 'dangerous' text that came his way at this time was a Hebrew translation of the gospels. 'I was very struck by reading this,' he wrote later, 'but was put off by all the miracles worked by Jesus.' (ND. I, 52) Obviously the extraordinary did not impress him greatly. He had ventured into forbidden territory! He had emerged from the ghetto but still was not at all happy to hear that his brother Samson, whom he greatly admired and respected, had become a Catholic. He did not hide his disappointment and let his older brother know how badly he felt. He accused Samson of changing religion in order to improve his position in the world and not from religious convictions.

We have but one letter from Jacob before he became a Catholic. It was written in January 1826 to Samson. In this letter we see him, now in his twenty-fourth year, trying to come to grips with a new world that he has begun to experience. There is something of the delayed adolescent to be found in his reasoning and attitude. He has begun to doubt, to question, but not yet to accept. And yet, one can see that the journey has begun. Where this might lead is not at all obvious. Freedom is seen as something of great importance, freedom to think, to reflect, and not to be enslaved by tradition – possibly a decadent tradition.

> God gave us power to think. This power should be put to use and not left idle. If one were to let the mind vegetate, if one were to surrender blindly to the bonds of religion, how would such a one differ from the brute beasts? Religion would turn him into what a beast is by nature. The reason why I have been given this gift is so that I might use it. (ND. I, 52-54)

He now comes to see that some forms of religion are enslaving and to be rejected. Freedom is to be treasured as a God-given gift. He has been in bondage all his life and now wants to make a breakthrough. This freedom is a requirement of true religion. It is a God-given gift to be used and not stifled. Religion seems to be opposed to freedom of thought; this is not acceptable. Jacob will choose to be free. In the same letter he goes on, questioning the Jewish religion that he was so steeped in up to now:

> How absurd it is to believe all the fables in the Bible ... What special attraction did God find in the Patriarchs? Was it that they had the true idea of the divine among a people who were in idolatry? Why did God not show the same interest in so many of the ancient philosophers? Can I possibly be unjust to think that God was still taking vengeance for the sin of Adam on all his posterity? We say that God chose the Jewish people to give them his holy laws. How can this choice be explained? Would it not be an injustice for God to choose just one race from among all the peoples of the earth and enlighten them and reveal to them the true principles of religion while leaving all others steeped in ignorance and idolatry? Were not other people God's creatures just like the

Israelites? From all this I come to the conclusion that what God requires of us is to recognise him, to be just and humane and that God chose Moses as a law-giver like any other law-giver. And furthermore, it matters little whether I be a Jew or Christian; what matters is that I adore God, whether in one person or in three. In any case, I assure you that I would be no better as a Christian than as a good Jew. (ND. I, 52-54)

The god that Libermann has difficulties with at this time is the god of vengeance, the tribal god who is concerned only with a particular tribe, the god who would not see anything of value in the philosophers but only in what is revealed in the Bible. This god is not to be accepted. So, Libermann takes the path of agnosticism. We see already that there is a missionary dimension in his thinking. All people are God's creatures; nobody is excluded from knowing God; all are called to worship God. The Jews cannot have a monopoly on God.

B. From the Ghetto to the Seminary

The journey from Saverne to Metz was also a journey from the narrow confines of rabbinical studies to a larger world. It was the first step away from Judaism. From Metz, Libermann moved to Paris. The reasons for this move are not clear. It would almost seem that he was looking for still wider horizons. Again, there was a spiritual and intellectual transformation. In Paris Jacob contacted David Drach who taught Hebrew in the Seminary of St Stanislaus. Drach arranged lodging for him in the college. He tells of how he felt in the seminary:

I got a place in St Stanislaus College. This was a time of extreme suffering for me. The experience of deep loneliness in that room where a single skylight enlightened the day; the thought of being away from my family, from my friends and from my homeland, all this brought on a deep depression. My heart was overcome by the most excruciating melancholy. It was then that I recalled the God of my fathers. I threw myself on my knees and prayed to be enlightened on the true religion. I asked him to let me know that if the beliefs of Christians were true I might know this, and if they were false I might reject them here and now. The Lord, who is near to all who call on him from their hearts, heard my prayer. Immediately I saw the light I came to see the truth. Faith entered my heart and my mind. I believed everything without any difficulty. All I wished from them was to be immersed in the waters of baptism. This joy was soon to be mine. I was prepared for this wonderful sacrament and was baptised on Christmas Eve. The same day I received the Holy Eucharist. I am truly astounded at the wonderful change that took place when the waters of baptism flowed over my forehead. All my doubts disappeared. The horror I felt for the priests' cassock now seemed to be quite different. Instead of being afraid, I was now attracted to it. I felt in a special way strength and courage to keep the law of the Christians. I felt a gentle attraction to everything concerning my new Faith. (ND. I, 65)

Francis Mary Paul Libermann was baptised on Christmas Eve, 1826. He remained on in St Stanislaus and began the study of philosophy. He was confirmed at Easter, and received the tonsure in June as a cleric of the diocese of Strasbourg. In October Drach again made arrangements for Libermann to be accepted into St Sulpice Seminary in Paris. This was one of the most prestigious seminaries in France at this time. The Superior, Garnier, like Drach, was a noted Hebrew scholar and this might have something to do with Libermann being accepted for priestly studies so soon after his conversion.

The peace and security that Libermann found in the seminary did not last for long.

Early in 1828 news of his conversion had reached his father in Saverne. Libermann received a letter from his father in which he was cursed, cut off from the family and now regarded as dead. This caused intense suffering. Now cut off from his family, he found support in the college community and soon was elected as a member of the Association of the Sacred Heart. This was a group of students, not more than nine members, who assembled regularly for prayer and to give each other mutual support. The need to be part of a group of like-minded people stayed with him and, as we shall see, influenced his missionary apostolate.

He received the Minor Orders in December 1828. In March of the following year he was to be ordained Subdeacon. On the eve of the ordination he had an epileptic seizure in the presence of his spiritual director. This constituted an impediment for advancement to Major Orders. He had nowhere to go. He was allowed to stay on in St Sulpice until 1831 and during this time he had five seizures. Hopes of ever being ordained seemed to vanish. At this time he was a cleric of the Archdiocese of Paris. It was arranged that he go to the Junior Sulpician house at Issy near Paris. He had no definite position there and for six years helped the Bursar of the College.

But there were other activities going on in the house. These are not as well documented. There is evidence of Libermann being involved with groups of students and in time becoming a kind of spiritual animator in some groups. It was usual for seminarians in St Sulpice and Issy to form pious associations. Libermann was a founder member of *Les Bandes de Pieté* and perhaps some other associations within the college. These groups caused some divisions among staff members of the college mainly because they were surrounded in secrecy. He seems to have had quite a major influence in the seminary through these groups. He was much appreciated and won the approval of the director, Fr Mollivault, who recommended him to the superior of the Eudist Congregation. This congregation was being reorganised at the time after being almost destroyed by the Revolution. The Eudists were looking for somebody to help in their novitiate in Rennes. In July 1837 Libermann joined the novitiate at Rennes with great enthusiasm and perhaps too much zeal. His role in the novitiate does not seem to be quite clear, but he had something to do with the formation of the novices. The Superior of the Eudists, Fr Louis de la Morinière, did not get on well with him. As usual in such a situation, this led to problems among the novices. Fr Louis, Libermann thought, was too authoritarian in his manner and wanted to control everything. Libermann disagreed about some works of the congregation that were not in line with its rules. This was not the only trouble.

One of Libermann's admirers in Issy, M. Brandt, joined the novitiate. Libermann was delighted at first but after some time he had reasons for regret. He found that during prayers and other religious exercises Brandt slept or sat laughing or making others laugh. He often engaged in pranks before the Blessed Sacrament. This whole affair seemed to Libermann to be malicious and even inspired by the devil. This, and similar problems in the novitiate, caused considerable distress for Libermann. He saw his work as useless and maybe harmful. He was torn by doubts. His epilepsy returned. He is near to despair. He may have been tempted to suicide. He has come to realise that a seminary or novitiate does not, of itself, produce sanctity. His state of mind he describes at this time before a new way opens up to him:

> In sincere truth I'm a useless instrument in the Church of God. Here I find myself like a piece of decayed wood. I am like one paralysed who wants to move but cannot. Yes! I have projects, and great ones but all to no effect. All that I can hope for now is a Christian death. The years pass, death is approaching, and still there are so many souls to be saved. (LS. II, 294)

'The many souls to be saved' seem to be what saved Libermann at this time of doubt and depression. In February 1838 he had a major seizure in the presence of the novices. This was particularly humiliating and affected his relations with the novices.

In August he had a visit from a Frederic Le Vavasseur, a Creole from the island of Bourbon in the Indian Ocean (now Reunion). Le Vavasseur he had known in St Sulpice where he was part of the *Bandes de Pieté*. They spent some time together and discussed the condition of the slaves in Bourbon where Frederic's family were slave owners. The evangelisation of the slaves was a concern of Le Vavasseur. The issue of slavery was a hot political one at the time and involved heated discussions in the Chamber of Deputies. The troubles of the small novitiate community are put into context when Libermann looks out from his little ghetto and sees the world around him.

Le Vavasseur continued in his campaign for the evangelisation of slaves. He drew up a memorandum on the subject for the superior of St Sulpice early in 1839. With another seminarian,

Eugene Tisserant, he brought the issue to the attention of Fr Desgenettes the parish priest of Our Lady of Victories in Paris. Both seminarians wrote to Libermann outlining their project for the apostolate to the slaves.

Le Vavasseur was born in Reunion (then Bourbon) in 1811. His parents were rich landowners and had slaves to work in their farms. Like most children of the settlers, he was sent abroad for studies. He had problems with the life of a student and had a breakdown at the *Ecole Polytechnique*. He began to study law, but again his health failed. Then, to the annoyance of his family, he entered St Sulpice seminary. The question of slavery was being very much discussed at the time, and Le Vavasseur had personal experience of slaves. An apostolate to the slaves took his attention at this time, and he consulted Libermann.

Tisserant, too, had some interest in the lot of slaves. He was born in Paris in 1814. His father had been governor of a province in the island of Haiti. His mother was born in Haiti. The family had to leave Haiti when it became independent from France in 1804. His mother was a very pious woman and devoted to the poor. Eugene was admitted to St Sulpice but had to leave because of failure in the examinations. He entered a Cistercian monastery, but soon left it. He was readmitted to St Sulpice in 1836.

We could say that the beginning of Libermann's missionary apostolate began with his correspondence with Le Vavasseur and Tisserant in the spring of 1839. He encourages the seminarians but advises caution. There is no evidence at this time of his willingness to be involved in any capacity other than as an interested adviser. During the summer vacation Libermann spent some time with them at Issy and together they organised 'L'Oeuvre des Noirs' (Project for the Blacks) and at least 6 other seminarians joined in the project. One of those, Maxime de la Brunier, was quite different from the two pioneers. He was bright, balanced and in the ecclesiastical world well-connected. His uncle was bishop of Mende. He was the leader of the group and we find him later accompanying Libermann to Rome and providing the expenses for the journey. Another, Jean Luquet was also intelligent, diplomatic and idealistic. He did not

continue with the group and later became a missionary in India
with the Society of French Foreign Missionaries. From there he
was sent to Rome to present the findings of a local synod. He
remained in Rome and had contact with Libermann later. He
became Libermann's source of information and advice on
matters concerning Rome.

In St Sulpice, one of the priests, Pinault, encouraged those
who were in the Project. An apostolate to the slaves seemed to be
in line with the gospel. Libermann was drawn into the Project. At
first he cautioned prudence – not surprisingly, in view of the
mental and emotional state of some of the members. He
considered it might be a suitable apostolate for the Eudist
congregation but had to abandon the idea because of his
relations with the superior of the Eudists. One piece of advice
that Libermann gave from the beginning and that he adhered to
later was that any apostolate of this kind should be undertaken,
not by individuals but by a community, well organised and
unified. How this could be formed was not yet clear. Libermann
returned to the novitiate in Rennes in September, seemingly
with the intention of continuing on there. But the seeds were
sown for a different apostolate for him. We now try and sketch
how this developed.

C. Conversion to Mission

It is worth considering Libermann as undergoing a second
conversion when he got involved in the Project.[2] On 28 October
1839, Libermann seems to have had a significant religious
experience. He described it in low-key fashion, but it was a
turning point in his life. He was doing a Novena before the feast
of the Apostles, Simon and Jude (October 28) when:

> The Good Lord gave me a little light which I cannot share
> with you (Le Vavasseur) for the present. I prefer to let the
> experience ripen before God, so that if it should please His
> Divine Goodness, and His Beloved Son, the little spark might
> become a brighter light. (ND. I, 661)

2. Bernard A. Kelly, *Life Began at Forty. The Second Conversion of Francis
Libermann C.S.Sp.*, Paraclete Press, Dublin, 1983. This gives a scholarly
analysis of Second Conversion, its importance for spiritual life and
shows how it is found in the case of Libermann.

The 'little spark' developed quickly, and six weeks later Libermann set out for Rome to do something for the slaves. With him on his way to Rome was the most promising seminarian in the Project, de la Brunnier. But he was to abandon Libermann later in Rome when the case seemed hopeless. Libermann's letter from Lyons, when he was on his way to Rome, gives us a glimpse of his conversion to the missionary apostolate. He writes to his brother trying to explain the decision to him, but finds it very hard to do so. He is happy with the decision but realises that it is a risk he is taking.

> I may be laughed at, despised, and even persecuted. Don't be afraid, don't worry. I assure you that I am the happiest man in the world, because, having nothing, I have God. (LS, II, 301)

A few days later, to a faithful confidant, Fr Carbon, he wrote: 'I could not resist the burning desire that kept nagging me all the time to do something for the glory of Our Lord. The decision was that I should leave. I left'. (ND. I, 676) This was a moment-ous decision.

Pierre Blanchard has written two volumes on Libermann's spirituality.[3] It is a work of profound learning and painstaking research. However, what seems strange is that the 'Second Conversion' does not seem to feature. It can be argued that Libermann's spirituality was influenced in a very significant way when he left the novitiate and set out to begin an apostolate for the slaves. It could well be that Libermann's spirituality took a very radical turn when he looked out into the world and saw the horror of slavery and meditated on the suffering of the slaves. But this is not our concern here. However, it has to be emphasised that mission does affect spirituality, and spirituality impacts on mission. Conversion to mission is a conversion in the realm of spiritual discernment and evangelical living. To have neglected the issue of slavery, to ignore such a moral and social question, would indicate a defect in spirituality, a kind of 'ghetto spirituality' that distorts the gospel. Libermann had moved away from this and had come to embrace mission spirituality.

---

3. *Le Vénérable Libermann*, Vol 1 *Son Expérience – Sa Doctrine*, Vol II *Sa Personalité – Son Action* (Desclée de Brouwer, 1946)

On 1 December 1839 Libermann departed from Rennes. Two days later came the Apostolic Constitution *In Supremo Apostolatus* of Pope Gregory XVI condemning the slave trade and slavery. Later that month a circular from the Ministry of Religious Affairs to the Bishops of France requested priests to be sent to the French colonies. Libermann arrived in Rome on 6 January and had an audience with the Pope in mid-February that was arranged by Drach. He got some encouragement from the Pope and set about writing a memorandum for *Propaganda Fide*. This was sent to the secretary of the Congregation at the end of March. A reply from *Propaganda* came in June. This was generally positive but had a condition that Libermann or the leader should be a priest. In the meantime Libermann composed a provisional rule for the Congregation of the Holy Heart of Mary, and a commentary on the rule. He then set about writing a commentary on the Gospel of John which he did not complete. In December the Coadjutor Bishop of Strasbourg agreed to ordain him.

Back in France Le Vavasseur was ordained priest. A newly appointed Vicar Apostolic for the island of Mauritius, Edward Collier, showed interest in the Project, and was looking for missionaries. Tisserant was ordained also that year.

Early in 1841 Libermann gets back to France and enters the seminary in Strasbourg to prepare for ordination. A friend of his from St Sulpice and Rennes, de Brandt, a nephew of the Bishop of Amiens is named Vicar General to Bishop Collier and he arranges to have Libermann ordained in Amiens where he and Le Vavasseur are setting up a novitiate for the new congregation. Libermann comes to Amiens and is ordained there on 13 September 1841. On 27 September the novitiate is opened at La Neuville near Amiens. A fragile foundation is laid for a formidable missionary project.

Reflection

Libermann was born into a very religious family. For twenty years he conformed to what was expected of a pious Jew in a Jewish ghetto. Social and political events led to the opening of the ghetto and with the collapse of that structure, widespread defections from Judaism resulted. Libermann and his brothers are typical of the change in religious belief and practice; his father typifies those who resist change and depend on a ghetto for security.

Most Irish Catholics grew up in a religious church-going environment. It was an environment very much protected by the political and ecclesiastical establishment. This became unstable in a changing society and the religious ethos was seriously threatened. The younger generation moved out. Church leaders tried to protect the structures. This is where we are.

Libermann had experienced living in an environment where Jews were regarded as racially inferior and unworthy of participating in the life of 'normal' humans. What enabled him to get out of this were the changes brought about by the French Revolution at one level and events in his personal life. The social condition of slaves was not the same as for Jews of course but degrees of social exclusion applied in both cases. The freedom enjoyed by the freed slaves was severely curtailed also. The time had come for change but the direction it might take was not clear.

The student protests beginning in France in 1968 echoed around the world. It was basically a time of questioning authority and leadership. In church affairs the Second Vatican Council had asked for change at the top. The encyclical *Humanae Vitae* of 1968 seemed to resist the way society was moving and sparked off widespread dissent and defections from the church. The mood among the leadership was for maintaining the *status quo*. Mission was for others, it was thought, and so opportunities were missed. In France Libermann listened to the debates regarding slavery and projects being discussed by some seminarians. Then he 'launched out into the deep'. In Ireland the missionary movement by-passed the church and was taken up by philanthropic Non-Governmental Organisations.

CHAPTER TWO

The Road to Freedom

a. Caring for Slaves

Libermann's mission originally was to the slaves in French territories. This would be extended as opportunities arose. In reaching out to slaves he was entering into areas where many issues were operating; he was entering a field where big business was being carried out by companies closely connected with the political authority. The French had their chief trading centre in Gorée, an island off the coast of Senegal. The *Compagnie de Senégal* had a monopoly here and had contracted to send 2,000 slaves every year to the French islands of the Caribbean and to Guyana.

The trade was regulated at one time according to the *Code Noir* drawn up by Colbert and issued in 1685 by Louis XIV. This contained the 'King's edict concerning the discipline of the church and state and the status of slaves in the islands of America'. Among its sixty articles we find that slaves are property, the masters are responsible for seeing that they are baptised, instructed in the faith and kept alive. Theft is punishable by death, fugitives when captured are to be executed, or in the case of short absence, have their ears cut off. Slaves were exempt from work on Sundays and Feast Days. This concession no longer applied in the nineteenth century. By that time movements for the liberation of slaves had gained momentum. Slaves were getting some concessions and a limited freedom. Slave trading was outlawed in France in 1848.

In 1840 it was reported to *Propaganda Fide* that the territories of Martinique, Guadeloupe, Bourbon and Guyana had a total of 251,971 slaves and 12,447 emancipated black people. Signs of unrest were seen to give warning of anarchy. The French Minister for the Navy sent out an appeal to the bishops of France to supply more priests for these territories overseas. The missionaries were needed to 'moralise' and control the emancipated ones.

The supply of missionaries for the French colonies was provided mainly by the Seminary of the Holy Spirit. The seminary, founded in 1703, had gone through a very difficult time during the French Revolution when most religious institutes were suppressed. In 1805 Napoleon allowed some missionary institutes to re-open. He put these under the control of the Ministry of Religious Affairs. Co-operation between church and state was further enhanced with the restoration of the monarchy in 1814. The king was soon asking missionary institutions to provide priests for the colonies and they re-opened seminaries and continued to supply the colonies and other mission areas with personnel. The missionaries received support from the government which was quite substantial. It meant, however, that there was tight control and with a few exceptions the priests were mainly concerned with ministry to the French colonists and administrators. Little attention was given to the slaves or to former slaves.

b. Abolitionist Movements in Britain

The abolitionist movements were spearheaded mainly by the Quakers in America and in Britain. In the mid-eighteenth century the Quakers in Philadelphia had taken a stand against slavery that had already been condemned by George Fox in 1670. John Wesley's *Thoughts on Slavery* (1714) made a significant social and political impact. In the second half of the 18th century some voices in France, America and Scotland were raised against the trade. Most mainline churches regarded slavery as a matter of life that was taken for granted. The Quakers, Anthony Benezet in Philadelphia and Granville Sharp in Britain, played an enormous role in bringing the issue into the political forum. The abolitionists were a tiny minority but showed extraordinary commitment to highlighting the evils of slavery. The European economy greatly benefited from slavery and it was regarded as a necessary part of the socio-economic system of the time. It is surprising to find the Founding Fathers of the United States insistent on maintaining slavery. Jefferson, Washington and Madison were slave owners. It wasn't unusual for religious communities to own slaves.

In Britain Granville Sharp was practically a lone voice but he persisted in sending petitions and circulating pamphlets. His campaign gained considerable momentum, with the Zong case getting wide publicity. This concerns a certain Captain Collingwood, captain of a Liverpool slave ship who ordered 133 slaves to be thrown overboard to help the others to survive when supplies were dangerously low. Collingwood took the case to court to claim insurance for the loss of the slaves. This caused widespread revulsion and brought the issue more to the fore in 1783. Sharp was joined by Thomas Clarkson, a deacon of the Anglican Church. His *Essay on Slavery and Commerce of the Human Species* had considerable effect and brought the young MP William Wilberforce into the anti-slavery campaign. Wilberforce campaigned vigorously for abolition of slavery and after several setbacks eventually got parliament to ban the slave trade in 1807.

c. Abolition in France

The abolitionist movements in France were quite different from those in Britain. Prior to the French Revolution some liberals and the Enlightenment writers railed against the practice of slavery. Slavery in the French territories was banned in 1794 but this ban was revoked by Napoleon in 1802. Abbé Gregoire (1750-1831), a constitutional bishop, was the most prominent advocate for abolition during his lifetime. He had many of the pamphlets of Sharp and Clarkson translated and distributed. He was seen as not being quite in tune with the hierarchy throughout the campaign. The liberals and the Enlightenment writers who campaigned for abolition were generally strongly opposed to the Catholic Church and were anti-clerical. The attacks on the Jesuits and their expulsion from France prior to the Revolution meant that the church had battles to wage on many fronts and would have found it hard to join with the abolitionist movements. Moreover, no clear directions were coming from the papacy. The slave revolts and the terrible massacres in San Domingo during the first years of the nineteenth century caused such revulsion that the case for abolition was weakened in the eyes of many who might previously have been supportive.

A royal decree of 1817 forbade the importation of slaves into the French colonies. However, this was not followed up with any great enthusiasm. In 1820 a dispute arose about slavery in the West Coast of Africa. Morenas, an agent of Gregoire, accused the Governor General of Senegal, Schmaltz, of protecting slave traders. Morenas later published a short history of the slave trade, a well documented work that had quite a degree of success in raising the consciousness of people on the issues. The revolution in 1830 and the accession of Louis Philippe to the throne advanced the cause of the abolitionists. Between 1830 and 1841 laws were enacted to make it easier for slaves to procure their freedom. More than 40,000 slaves in Guadeloupe and Martinique got their freedom during that time. This led to social chaos.

Slaves were not prepared for freedom and the social and economic fabrics of the colonies seemed to be threatened. Accordingly, the French government wanted to promote a programme of moral, religious and social instruction. Money was made available to priests, brothers and sisters who would undertake this ministry in the colonies. To streamline this operation from the point of view of the priests, the government gave exclusive rights to the Seminary of the Holy Spirit to prepare, vet and send priests to the colonies. But the seminary charged with providing the clergy was under attack. The internal structure was greatly flawed and so it had little control over the priests being sent. From outside it was being harshly criticised for not being sufficiently involved in promoting the welfare of slaves and former slaves. In 1845 the great liberal Catholic, Montalambert, made a vicious attack on the seminary in parliament. Morale was low and political pressure was being put on the church and the king to deal more effectively with the slave issue. After the fall of the monarchy the trading was banned in 1848.

d. Slave Revolts
The fight against the slave trade and slavery was not confined to the political and social forces that were operating for freedom for slaves. Two factors need to be considered also. Firstly, the slave trade had become less profitable. The slaves in the Americas had become numerous as more and more were brought in. Added to this was the fact that Europe was not as dependent on goods

from America as previously. So the demographic and economic realities fed into a decline of interest in the trade.

The slaves themselves and those who were freed played an important role in the process of liberation. Just as the colonial powers did not just give independence to their colonies in the 1950s and 1960s, but the colonised countries themselves fought for freedom and independence, so the descendents of Africans bought into slavery played a very significant role in the process of liberation. This is an aspect that is not sufficiently taken into consideration in the context of abolition. Those who campaigned on behalf of the slaves are rightly given recognition, but the efforts of the slaves themselves and their descendents are often ignored.

Slave owners were in dread of violence breaking out especially in the case of domestic slaves. The slaves did not always patiently endure the ill-treatment meted out to them and individuals and groups revolted with passion. Slave revolts took place in the islands of Antigua as early as 1735, in Jamaica in 1760 and again in 1831 and in Grenada in 1795. The slaves were not just objects to be liberated; they raised their voices before many of the famous abolitionists spoke out in their favour. However, the revolution of slaves in Haiti, which began in 1792 and led to independence for the country in 1804, had particular significance. The emergence of Haiti as the first black republic outside Africa challenged slavery as an institution. The revolt in Haiti was the only successful one and it sent shock waves through slave-owning communities in the Americas and Caribbean. We shall see that it had particular significance for Libermann who later had correspondence with Isaac Louverture, the son of the leader of the Haitian revolt. This revolt influenced Libermann's thinking.

A number of revolts took place in North America. In 1800 a slave, Gabriel Prosser made elaborate plans to capture the town of Richmond in Virginia and had thousands of slaves on his side, some who were armed with guns. He was betrayed by two of his followers before the attack took place and he and many of his followers were hanged. Denmark Vesey in 1821 was able to organise a system of revolutionary cells. His movement was inspired by biblical events which to him and his followers justified blood-shedding on a massive scale. A day before the

revolution was to take place in Charlestown, he too was
betrayed and brutal reprisals followed. Vesey and his followers
were hanged. The revolt of Nat Turner in 1831 in Virginia was
also a kind of religious crusade. His vision was more apocalyptic
and he focused it on Jerusalem in Virginia which was to become
the New Jerusalem. Beginning with the massacre of his master's
entire family, he and his followers went through the area by
night and brutally killed the inhabitants who were slave
owners. He was prevented from entering Jerusalem and was
later captured and hanged. This revolt was widely reported.
The brutality exercised by Turner and his men terrorised the
white communities and showed the anger and vengeance that
lay beneath the seemingly subservient slaves.

Coming to the time Libermann began his mission, 1839, a
significant event happened in New York. A boat, *Amistad*,
sailing from Cuba with slaves on board, had its crew, with the
exception of the captain and first mate, murdered by the slaves
led by a man named Cinque. He demanded that the Africans be
returned to Africa but the boat went to New York. There the
leaders were put on trial and were defended by John Quincy
Adams. The court held that the murder was justified. For the
first time, America applied to slaves the same right to revolt as
they believed they themselves had.

e. Church and Liberation

As we have seen, just at the time when Libermann set out for
Rome to seek approval for his mission, Pope Gregory XVI roundly
condemned slavery and the slave trade. Gregory became pope in
1831, a time of considerable crisis for the papacy. For some time
discontent was brewing within the Papal States and throughout
Italy for reform. This was spearheaded by the *Carbonari*, a secret
society strongly influenced by the Freemasons. Gregory was
involved in a rearguard action to maintain his authority over
these states. He did all in his power to oppose the movements
for change and for a unified Italy and this depleted the finances
of the papacy. He opposed all innovations, even the construction
of railways.

Conservative at home, Gregory was passionate about
extending the mission of the church abroad. He had come to the

papacy from *Propaganda Fide* and showed great support for mission activity. He strove to unlink the mission of the church from that of the governments. He favoured building up of native clergy and strengthening the independence of the churches from government interference. During his pontificate 70 new missionary dioceses were set up and 195 missionary bishops appointed.

Prepared to extend the territorial boundaries of the church, Gregory was less prepared to move in social and political matters. A serious conflict had arisen in France. A group had formed around a priest, Lamennais, and his publication *L'Avenir*, that was strongly opposed to the alliance of throne and altar, as it was called. The group met with opposition from the French bishops and appealed to Rome. They got a frosty reception from the pope. Shortly afterwards their project, though not explicitly named was solemnly condemned in an encyclical, *Mirari Vos*, which condemned the 'indifferentism and that absurd and erroneous doctrine that freedom of conscience is to be claimed and defended for all men'.

f. Missionary Expansion

The period between the French Revolution and the First World War was a time when European influence spread throughout the world. Political authority, social prestige, cultural eminence and religious influence were exercised by Europe. Political and commercial ambition combined with evangelical zeal influenced whole regions up to then almost completely unknown in Europe. Catholic missionary advance was closely allied with the political expansionism of Spain and Portugal. In Africa the Capuchin mission in the Congo gave bright promise. During the second half of the 17th century 600,000 Africans were baptised. However, the evangelisation of the Africans was truly deplorable. In 1650 *Propaganda Fide* instructed that people might be baptised *in fide ecclesiae* like children and those not in their right mind. Not surprisingly by the 1840s the whole project was in ruins. Nothing of any significance was achieved until the nineteenth century.

The missionary revival in the nineteenth century, with which we are more directly concerned, was greatly influenced by ideological and commercial developments in Europe – the home base for missionary activity. The role of Pope Gregory XVI, first as Prefect of *Propaganda Fide* and then as pope did a lot to change the situation. Rome began to exercise stricter control over ecclesiastical affairs. New religious congregations were founded in the nineteenth century and most of these were missionary. 25 of these approved by Rome were of French origin and as many more from outside France were approved. Another development of importance was the involvement of new congregations of brothers and sisters. In areas that concerned Libermann, the Brothers of the Christian Schools opened a school in Reunion in 1817 and the Ploemel Brothers had a school in Senegal in 1840. Mother Javouhey, foundress of the Sisters of St Joseph of Cluny, had ongoing correspondence with Libermann. The Cluny Sisters were in Reunion, Senegal and French Guyana in the 1820s.

Libermann's mission was but one among many missionary enterprises within the church of his time. The missionary élan came mostly from religious societies with members from rural backgrounds. The secular powers no longer engaged in spreading the gospel. Rome played the part of co-ordinating and directing and encouraging. The older religious orders were still playing a significant part that was to continue.

The foundation in Lyons of the *Association for the Propagation of the Faith* in 1822 by Pauline Jaricot marked a significant break with the past. Founded by a lay woman it limited its role to fundraising and did not send missionaries overseas. By providing financial support for missionaries it meant that they could be more independent of the governments. By 1846 it was raising 3.5 million francs per year in 400 dioceses in Europe and America. The appeal was principally to middle class Catholics. It helped to create a missionary consciousness over a broad area that helped the mission of the church and the missionary societies to reach out throughout the world.

g. Protestant missions
Until the close of the eighteenth century Protestant missionary movements were almost entirely confined to the policy of the *Society for the Propagation of the Gospel* founded in 1701 to assist

'our loving subjects in foreign parts from falling prey to atheism, infidelity, popish superstition and idolatry'. The coming into being of the Baptist Missionary Society in 1792, the London Missionary Society in 1795, the Church Missionary Society in 1799, the British foreign Bible Society in 1804 and other initiatives heralded a new era in Protestant expansion that had a knock-on effect in Catholic circles. Germany, Switzerland and Holland contributed greatly to the Protestant advance.

A part of the campaign of the British anti-slavery movements was the repatriation of former slaves to Africa. In 1887 a total of 411 slaves were to be repatriated to Sierra Leone but only 130 survived the journey. The venture was a failure but it focused attention on the African continent. Later, Clarkson organised 1,200 to be brought from Nova Scotia to Sierra Leone. The American *Colonisation Society*, founded in 1816 proposed the idea of colonies in Africa for liberated black people. This led to the Republic of Liberia being formed. Those being repatriated were usually accompanied by Protestant missionaries. As in the case of abolition, the Catholics were to follow the Protestant initiatives.

This was a stimulus for Catholics to get involved. The challenge was taken up in 1834 at the Second Council of Baltimore which sought volunteers for Liberia. Two Irish-born priests, Edward Baron and John Kelly, volunteered and arrived in West Africa in January 1840. This venture, as we shall see, is intimately connected with that of Libermann's. After contact had been established between Libermann and Barron, the focus of Libermann's attention shifted from the islands to the West Coast of Africa. It was from there that millions of people had been sent into slavery across the Atlantic.

Reflection
For a variety of reasons slavery was outlawed by the 1840s. Why did it last for so long and why was it practised to such an extent by Christians and Christian countries? It was, of course a very profitable business and its abolition was as much a matter of economic interests as of humanitarian considerations.

As might be expected the abolitionists were not from the social or political establishments, nor were mainline churches actively engaged in the movements. In France especially, the Enlightenment writers, critics of the Catholic hierarchy, were abolitionists. The power of the anti-slavery campaign came from its moral stance. Economic and political 'realities' can suppress awareness of patent injustices. Truth prevails eventually. Hostile critics can be true friends!

The effects of the inhuman practice could not be eradicated by passing laws and forming resolutions of good intent. The Jewish ghettos could be demolished, but the Jews remained stigmatised. They were to find that liberation brought even heavier burdens onto their race. The descendants of the slaves remained a despised people. The African people in their homeland were seen as ancestors of slaves. As one who had found true freedom in Jesus Christ, Libermann's lived experience was to point out the way to be followed.

Slaves were capital used by rich individuals and companies for profit. Fortunately this perception has changed with the general acceptance of basic human rights. The capitalist ideology is still very powerful and can be operating in 'free' and freedom-loving countries. In times of progress and prosperity abuses are often ignored or even justified on the grounds of profit. Ireland has passed through a time of economic prosperity, this has come to an end and questions are being raised about policies and practices of the 'good times'.

It is too soon for an assessment to be made on how Ireland in prosperous times treated immigrants and migrant workers. The change in the economy has an effect on the social scene. The church's contribution in promoting social justice appears positive but the problems are new and the challenge not yet defined. Where the unemployment figures are dangerously high, social cohesion can suffer.

The church has a role to play but is pre-occupied by other matters. The fact that lay women and men are taking a more active part in church affairs is a positive sign but the missionary dynamic should be applied. That means the Christian community is involved in social and political life and so it is concerned with promoting justice. To baptise slaves and see to it that they go to Mass on Sundays could not be acceptable as pastoral ministry.

CHAPTER THREE

Called to Mission

In the course of the year 1839, one issue dominated Libermann's thought. He had been consulted by the seminarians who were trying to do something to help the slaves in the French colonies. He had taken the suffering of the slaves to heart, and to help them would be his major preoccupation for the rest of his life. As we have seen, the challenge came from seminarians who sought advice from Libermann about their project. In encouraging the seminarians he became more and more involved in the work that was being proposed and his first advice is from a man who is obviously a deeply spiritual person and a practical one as well.

> Our Lord wishes something to be done for the salvation of these poor people who have been neglected for so long. I advise you to continue with your project for the love of the Lord Jesus. I recommend that you take on this wonderful work and get involved in a serious way. But do not depend on yourselves or on your own plans. Do not try to persuade anyone, do not force anyone, but let the Lord of the harvest do his work. It is for him to choose the workers he wishes to send into the harvest. (LS. IV, 1)

Faced with a seemingly impossible task and resources that were far from adequate, Libermann is in a waiting mode. The project is laudable but the means are not available. He is not put off by difficulties but waits for a way to open up. Mission begins from a position of weakness. Its strength comes from the Holy Spirit. The power of the Spirit is manifest in weakness. The mission of the church is in the real world, it is true. But the success of a Christian mission does not depend on political patronage, on financial backing nor even on human talents alone. What is primary is that it conforms to the mission initiated and passed on by Jesus Christ. In proclaiming the kingdom of God, Jesus did not rely on political or economic powers. Good intentions were not enough; the mission that was proposed had to be examined in a serious and practical manner. The spiritual, the emotional and the material had to be taken into consideration.

The crisis in mission usually arises from within a church or a congregation that is rich, comfortable, settled in its ways and content to give its surplus to the beggars at the gate. It would seem that Libermann had become keenly aware of his own weakness, his physical condition as an epileptic, his social condition as a cleric barred from advancement to the priesthood and his troubles with the novices he was dealing with at this juncture. Weakness is not an excuse for inaction, but neither is it a motive for precipitous action. The Spirit in strange ways has to enter into the planning. This has to be taken into account and one must be realistic about the consequences of going against the tide and not conforming to conventional wisdom. So he warns the young men:

> In everything you do you will be regarded as stupid, imprudent and proud. All sorts of such compliments will be paid to you. When people see the insurmountable difficulties that, humanly speaking, face the project, they will see it as an impossible venture. Those who do not experience the action of God within themselves promoting such a project will see it as impossible because of all the difficulties. (LS. IV 2)

Jesus was tempted to use extraordinary means to promote his mission. He rejected these and chose the path of weakness, of suffering and of failure as the world judges. At the start of his mission, Jesus chose companions to share in his mission. His choice of companions might not seem to be ideal. He set out from a position of weakness and fragility. The strength of the mission then was in the spirit of community that Jesus built up that was particularly evident in what is called 'table fellowship'. The weakness of the missionary is an experience that has to be shared. The work of the mission is the work of a community – a community that is often weak and powerless. The future missionaries were advised:

Whatever turn the project may take, one thing is essential. You must live in a community that is carefully established. Pride and intransigence would destroy all the good you might hope to achieve. It is much better to have a few than a large disunited group. (LS. IV, 8)

The dynamism comes from a spirit that brings people together in unity that inspires them with faith and hope and love. What is to be feared is pride, the superiority complex that seeks to conquer and dominate. Again, it is from personal experience that Libermann came to realise the need for community in a mission apostolate. Just before taking the definitive move that involved him in the new adventure, he finds that he is called to a difficult apostolate and ill-equipped for it.

This is the state of mind of Libermann when he is on the threshold of launching a missionary movement. He does not see himself as a hero; he is overcome by a sense of powerlessness to such an extent that what he wants is only 'to be buried in a tomb and not to get out from it, if that were the will of God' and yet, from utter helplessness comes mysterious courage and purpose: 'I could not resist the longing that urged me constantly to do something for the glory of Our Lord. The decision was that I leave, and I left.' (LS. I, 676)

Leaving the security of Rennes was the action that confirmed the missionary vocation. It would seem to be a foolish decision. He had nothing to recommend him for the project he was undertaking. The utter poverty of the missionary is now combined with a joyful determination to do something for the wretched of the earth. On his way to Rome he wrote to his brother, Samson:

I have left Rennes. Now I have nobody on earth to depend on. I have nothing. I don't know what will become of me. I will be taken for a man who is insane; I will be despised, and possibly persecuted. Don't worry, don't be anxious. I am the happiest man in the world for I have nothing but God alone. (LS. II, 301)

This letter shows a wonderful sense of freedom – the freedom of one who has left everything to follow the prompting of the Spirit. Libermann has escaped from the structure that held him prisoner in one sense but had formed him as did the 'hidden life' of his Master and Lord. He is free – free even from the worries of one who has nothing for his long journey to Rome. Like the father of his race, the frail Jew had left his country and his father's house for a land that will be shown him. His mission for the present is to get approval from Rome for his project. His mission is not an individual enterprise. It is the mission of the church. He needs to have that link with the church authorities otherwise the mission would not have the authenticity required by a church mission.

On his way to Rome, he wrote a letter which could be regarded as one of the most important of his life. It outlines the essence of his theology of mission. It is not, however, a theological work. It is really the outpouring of his heart provoked by a remark that was made about him. A distinguished cleric, a spiritual director of a seminary, Feret, who once held Libermann in high esteem and consulted him about a problem of Jansenism in the diocese, was reported as having said that Libermann was leading some talented young men to be butchered in Africa. Now, Libermann expected criticism. He knew that he would be regarded as slightly out of his mind. Yet, when the criticism came, he did not take it lightly. The mission had to be defended. The staunch supporter of the ecclesiastical *status quo* was confronted head-on in a style and language that is not charact-eristic of Libermann. The main thrust of the letter is not merely a defence of his project, it is a scathing attack on the whole attitude of one who is seen as holding an important function in the diocese. This man has been directing young people. Libermann tells him that his approach is completely wrong:

> I do not at all agree with the way you give spiritual direction. It looks as if you want to set yourself up as one to decide on vocations. This is not a matter for the director at all. His role is to obey the will of God as revealed to the person. I notice you decide vocations on the basis of reason ... It is clear that what pertains to God and to the interior life should not be subjected to the examination of reason ... It is for the director to provide the conditions that will facilitate God's direction. A director with his own ideas, his own individual point of view, his own principles, often resists the working of the

Holy Spirit. It is not for you to draw boundaries or impose laws for Our Lord. (LS. II, 310)

The good, solid, dependable spiritual director is really taken to task. What is really in question is not merely a matter concerning spiritual direction as such. The real issue is whether the spiritual director has a truly missionary outlook. He seems to lack this, and hence, his whole approach is defective. 'The Spirit blows wherever it wills.' The structures claim definite ways of acting and thinking. The prisoner of the structures feels he must put down definite markers and chart clear routes for anyone aspiring to the priesthood. Libermann's method of spiritual direction, prior to his conversion to mission, was not much different from what is denounced here. He knows what he is talking about – the director who is expected to help people conform, rather than listen to the Spirit of God.

The accusation that talent is being squandered in Africa is not taken lightly. There is an unusual tone of vehemence and sarcasm in the reply to this. But again, this is not just self-defence. It is not the wrath of a hurt ego that is being voiced. It is the plea of a missionary for his adopted people:

So those who are fervent, generous and of good character should be kept in France while millions of poor and abandoned people are let go to hell, and when God has inspired people with generous disposition regarding these poor people. No! These poor souls should only have the rejects, the common ones, the defective, those who are good for nothing! This is not according to the will of God. The perspective of Our Lord is much wider than that. He has come to save all, the least as well as the greatest. Consequently, His priestly spirit is simply the spirit of reconciliation and salvation for the whole human race. And furthermore, those who have the fullness of the priesthood of their Master ought to extend their mercy to the whole world. They should not be misers by giving what is worthless. When Our Lord sent the great St Paul to the reprobate Gentiles, who would have required that great apostle be kept in Judea for the sake of the Chosen People? Of course, there were good reasons for believing that he

would have done more for his own people than for the
Gentiles.(LS. II, 307-318)

Having first of all questioned a fundamental distortion in the
approach to spiritual direction, Libermann then goes on to point
out that fidelity to the Spirit requires a 'Catholic' frame of mind.
Jesus' salvific mission was for all. Nobody is to be excluded.
Neither must some be considered second-class or worse.
Mission to the poor is not optional; it is not for those who may
not be well enough qualified for ministry in what are thought to
be the 'normal' situations. Jesus is the Universal High Priest. His
care must be extended to all. When reflecting on John's gospel
some months later, attention is focused on Jesus, the Good
Shepherd, as the One with a mission that is truly universal. And
this universal care for people is contrasted with Judaism that
excluded people from belonging to the fold:

> In the former church represented by the Synagogue, generally
> speaking, there were no sheep that could come to it or be
> united with it. But Our Lord wished to establish a universal
> fold. He calls in all the Gentiles and forms another fold. The
> new fold has its source in the first but now has its own
> existence and is not subject to what went before. The ancient
> fold was too small to embrace all the sheep and is terminated.
> The universality of the flock is now united in the fold that is
> formed by the Divine Shepherd himself. This fold is able to
> contain the whole flock and to provide for its subsistence.
> (Comm 510)

Libermann rarely refers to his Jewish past. When he does so
here, he wants to emphasise the universal nature of the church in
contrast to the exclusiveness of the Jewish religion. He has
experienced the life of the Synagogue and has left it behind, but
finds something similar in the church, or rather in the minds of
some who are more concerned with their little flock as to exclude
others. The antidote for such a mentality is found in fidelity to
the inspirations of the Holy Spirit. If the Spirit inspires people to
take on a mission, this must be respected. The prudence of the
worldly is contrary to the hope of the Christian. The church in its
infancy faced the issue of exclusiveness, and in the controversy
even Peter came in for rebuke by the mission-minded Paul. The

issue, once settled in principle, constantly needs to be revisited in order to be faithful to the universal mission of Jesus.

When he arrived in Rome Libermann presented a Memorandum to the secretary of *Propaganda Fide*, Mgr Cadolini. The purpose of this was to seek

> guidance and encouragement in carrying out God's will for a number of people who are profoundly touched by the terrible evils suffered by poor people in many countries and who wish to help them overcome the ignorance and vice they are steeped in. (ND. II, 68-76)

Two days after Libermann left Rennes for Rome, Pope Gregory XVI issued a Bull, *In Supremo Apostolatus*, in which he condemned slavery and the slave trade and gave 'a solemn warning to all Christians, that from now on no one dare to harass, abuse or despoil of his property or reduce anyone into slavery'. The time would seem to be judged perfectly for an apostolate to the slaves. Still, the response from the Secretary to Libermann was that since he was not a priest, his project could not be approved. Libermann's reaction to this is significant:

> I presented the Memorandum to the Secretary. He received me very coldly. His response always came back to the same thing, that since I was not a priest I could not think of carrying out this mission. This was the most painful response I could have been given. If the reply were a definite negative, I would have been happy, for I would have seen in it the message of God and would have withdrawn from the project there and then. I wanted to do the will of God, and that would be manifested to me by my superiors. I put forward my proposal. They knew what it contained and what should be done. (LS. II, 455-462)

For Libermann, the fact that he was not a priest was irrelevant as far as his mission was concerned. The question was whether or not the proposed mission was deserving of approval. Once again, he finds himself up against the exclusive mentality that has drawn boundaries and clearly indicated what is 'for priests only'. This mentality has to be challenged and was challenged. The Cardinal Prefect, Fransoni, was contacted. He encouraged Libermann 'and his friends to preserve and attend

to everything that would enable them respond to their vocation'.
(ND. II, 14) There was some hope still!

Encouragement came from another quarter. Bishop Collier
has been recently appointed to Mauritius. He hears of Libermann
and sees hope of getting help for his island Vicariate. He is
crying out for missionaries for his island diocese. Whereas in
Rome Libermann had found that 'The majority, and especially
the most pious among them and the most prudent had a very
bad opinion of me. They saw my proposal as inspired by
ambition and they had all sorts of suspicion' (LS. II, 456). In
contrast to some in Rome, a missionary bishop provided some
encouragement:

> He was concerned with his diocese, of course, but didn't try to
> oppose what was being proposed. He wished to be helped but
> did not give the impression of wanting everything done his
> own way. I found this attitude very wise indeed and have not
> found it anywhere else. Everyone seems to want things their
> way, and that is a sure way of impeding and even destroying
> God's work. It is best to let people go ahead without
> tormenting them or oneself as to whether they are right or
> wrong. Clearly they have little experience, but they will get this
> by God's grace if they have good will and will change their
> ideas when they see they are wrong. (ND. II, 85-88)

People in certain positions seem to think that they have a
monopoly of wisdom and can speak for God. Whether it is in
spiritual direction or in ecclesiastical bureaucratic positions,
there are those who want to dictate to others and to God! Where
there could be any danger, they will counsel doing nothing.
Then there are others, who look beyond the immediate horizons
and consider what the people need most, and these are not
afraid of mistakes; they are not put off by lack of experience.
Mission, of its nature, presumes inexperience. In many instances,
the greater sin is to do nothing rather than to make mistakes by
attempting to do the best one can in the circumstances. The
church is constantly called to move beyond maintenance to
mission. It must look beyond the immediate situation to the
world outside and must reach out to this world. Moral theology
has been often crippled by the mentality that wants security. It is

rendered decadent by holding on to outdated formulae when the world had moved ahead and new ways of life, new cultures and new problems cry out for solution. Solutions can only be arrived at by immersion in the situation and when, with complete fidelity to the gospel and to the church, one strives to bring about the new environment.

What Libermann wanted from Rome was approval and encouragement, as he said. He wanted approval for a community of priests that would, as he laid down in a draft rule, be totally devoted to the poorest and the most abandoned. His missionaries would be required:

> not to let pass any opportunity for doing good, not only spiritual but material as well. They (missionaries) must be the advocates, the supporters, the defenders of the weak and the powerless against those who oppress them. They will be especially kind to the most hardened sinners, to those damaged by illness and vice, to those who are most uncivilised, and those who oppose them. They will try to put into practice that beautiful counsel of St Paul to be all things to all so as to win all for Jesus Christ. They will put themselves at the service of all, striving to adapt to the tastes, desires, views and character of others so as to allow the love of the truths of the gospel to enter into the hearts of the people. (ND. II, 258-287)

One person sees the mission to Africa as sending people to their death. Another cannot see how a mission can be spearheaded by one who is not a priest. When one considers the above quotation, the extraordinary chasm between the different mentalities is manifest. People are not being sent to be butchered but to help their unfortunate brothers and sisters. Priesthood ought not to be considered solely as a status that is conferred on one, but as a mission that one undertakes, the mission of Jesus Christ 'to bring the Good News to the poor.' In commenting on Chapter 4 of John's gospel, Libermann makes the point that the first missionary of Jesus was the Samaritan woman! And indeed, Jesus' great missionary discourse follows on that meeting:

> That poor woman, wounded by sin and an outcast among her own people, an outsider and despised by the Jews, scarcely has she heard Jesus' discourse and must have understood but

very little of it, when the sinner becomes an apostle ... She runs
to announce the gospel to the inhabitants of the place ... she
would have left everything and followed him if he had called
her'. (Comm 123-125)

That the Samaritan woman could be regarded as an apostle,
was obviously a great source of encouragement for Libermann.
The outsider who met Jesus called her village to Jesus. But the
missionary role of the Samaritan is also underlined. When she
brought people to Jesus, she disappeared from the scene again.
It is the lot of the missionary to announce Jesus and then move
on. The role of the missionary is to bring people to Jesus; he is
but a messenger. Jesus alone is the One True Shepherd. The
missionary is not to take the place of Jesus by drawing people to
himself. This was a fault in the Old Testament times:

> Basically there is only one shepherd, Our Lord. There cannot
> be any other true shepherd. In the minds of the Jews there
> was more than one shepherd as there were more than one
> fold. The prophets were seen to be shepherds for God had
> given them various laws. Thus, Moses was the shepherd of
> the Jews. The Gentiles were of the flock according to the
> Jews, being children of Noah. Noah was their shepherd. The
> Jews were the children of Abraham and of Moses and the
> Gentiles children of Noah. These denominations are still
> found even today in their books. But in the New Law and in
> the new fold, such different denominations do not exist. All
> are directly and without distinction the flock of Our Lord,
> and receive from him, directly and uniquely the interior
> direction of grace and life. (Comm 515)

The fundamental task of the missionary is to bring people to
Christ. Significantly, when Libermann is having great difficulty
getting approval from Rome, he reflects on the Supreme Pastor,
Jesus Christ and realises that all – pope, bishops, priests *et al* – are
members of the flock of Jesus. 'The true pastors are at the same
time the shepherds and the sheep. Our Lord is the unique Pastor
and all other pastors are his sheep.' (Comm 489) One can almost
hear him reminding those who were holding up his project that
they too were members of the flock of Jesus. The notion of the
church as the People of God comes through here. All belong to

the fold. The rather strange reference to the universality that could be found among the Jews is not teased out, but one might wonder if such universality might be wanting in the church too.

The sheepfold has to remain open for all. Nobody ought to be excluded. Jesus calls all to enter and meet him and share his life. The black people have been excluded for so long, but their time has come. Why this exclusion? Why so late? Perhaps some light is thrown on this by Libermann as he meditates on Jesus driving the traders from the Temple. He remarked that Jesus went to the Temple every year, but only when he began his mission did he drive them out:

> During his hidden life, he wished to remain hidden and did not want to perform in public until the moment came for his public life. He shows us in this way that one ought not to set out to correct faults until one has authority for this from the Holy Spirit. (Comm 70)

The mission is a response to the Spirit in the face of evils in the world even if the evil has been there from time immemorial. At some stage the Holy Spirit inspires people to counter this evil. To gather together the children of God into the sheepfold of Christ, under the Supreme Shepherd, Jesus, this is the mission of the church. Slaves must not be slaves. They must be free and proud to be free. Libermann was challenged, and he overcame obstacles for the sake of those who cried out to be free. Although Libermann complained about some aspects of his reception in Rome, it would seem that he got quite a good response when all is taken into account. The fact that he got any response at all could be surprising. To have been able to speak with the pope shows considerable diplomatic aplomb on his part. This is characteristic of his subsequent apostolate.

While the greatest part of his work in Rome was negotiating with the authorities there, he still kept in mind those who had proposed this mission. Even when the prospects for authorisation were bleak he began to draft a Rule for *The Congregation of the Holy Heart of Mary*. The congregation is described as 'a community of priests who are sent by, and in the name of, Our Lord Jesus Christ to proclaim the gospel and establish his reign among the poorest and most abandoned in the church of God'. (ND. II, 336)

Both the proclamation and forming church communities are intimately connected. The methods to be followed in this work are set out in some detail. The titles of some chapters give some idea of how Libermann envisaged the mission. Chapter V is concerned with preaching, instructing and catechising, Chapter VI is on how the community is to remain in a place for sufficient time to carry out the catechesis. Chapter VIII deals with forming an indigenous clergy.

Conscious of his lack of knowledge of the mission territory, the people and the conditions the missionaries might have to face, he made it very clear that the Rule was provisional and not written in stone. The reason for drafting the Rule was simply: 'to give an impetus and a certain spirit to the work. Later changes can be made according to the experience that emerges.' (LS, 460) A few pointers towards the spirit and orientation of the community are given. 'The missionaries will let no opportunity pass in helping not only in matters spiritual but also in material matters ... They will be the advocates, the support and defenders of the weak and the little ones against all who oppress them ... They will patiently put up with the boorishness, faults and vices of the people and try to correct them with kindness and tenderness. (ND. II, 255-257)

Reflection

Libermann becomes involved in a vast and complex world. He was brought into it by young idealistic men who felt a desire to help the slaves. He sensed they lacked the ability to carry out their proposed mission. He experienced a clear call to lead the group and left the security of the seminary. This was a momentous decision that changed his spirituality and his apostolate. He founded a missionary society and pioneered a mission in Africa.

The Second Vatican Council presented a challenge to the Catholic Church to be renewed and renew the world. The church in Ireland seemed to be in a very healthy condition. Church attendance was outstanding, seminaries were full, religious sisters and brothers managed most secondary schools and most hospitals were efficiently run by sisters. The Council's call for renewal was for others and only in minor details for Ireland. This was a widely held view.

Irish society was not open to change. In social and religious affairs it was very conservative and insular. Censorship of books and films was very strict – ridiculously so at times. The Catholic hierarchy were a powerful force in social and political life. Prophetic voices went unheeded. Political leadership changed. Education at second level was made available for many more. Television began to open up a wider world. The revolution of the youth that began in France in 1968 spread and challenged the closed authoritarian establishment. Church attendance began to decline. Young idealistic people tended to volunteer for social development projects. Vocations to the priesthood and religious life fell dramatically.

Now in 2010, is Ireland a 'mission territory'? Is a mission to re-evangelise needed? Who are the 'slaves' of today ?

CHAPTER FOUR

A People as they are and as they ought to be

In the 1830s it could be said that there was a general consensus that slavery was immoral. What Libermann had to contend with was, granted that slavery is immoral, what could be done to the victims of the practice and the institution of slavery itself? Slavery raised the question of the European attitude and behaviour towards the African people. It posed a question for Christians who ought to regard all humans as children of God and all people entitled to certain basic human rights. As we have seen, individuals and groups outside the Catholic Church were actively involved in opposing slavery. A statement had been made by the Pope in 1839 that required a follow-through in action to bring about a radical change in the thinking and the behaviour of many Catholics. With very little by way of resources Libermann set about organising a mission that would attempt to heal the wounds inflicted on black people.

One need not expect to find any great depth in the theology and missiology of Francis Libermann. This is not being looked for here. What one finds is a practical concern for people in dire need. This brings with it dynamism and a practical programme that ought to be part and parcel of moral discourse. When it is said that slavery is immoral, surely then the consequence of this is to see what can be done. The practical steps that need to be taken enter into the moral equation. Obviously, it is possible to counter immoral behaviour by immoral means. So the whole dynamic in combating slavery and assisting those who have been victims of the practice has profound moral implications. The slavery issue in the first half of the nineteenth century might be compared with that of nuclear war today. Such a war is immoral. But what can be done?

It has to be remembered that there were very many who made profit from the slave trade and from the exploitation of slaves in the middle of the nineteenth century. Many were still gaining handsomely from the business. From the enormous expansion of this trading in human beings in the seventeenth and eighteenth centuries some people had acquired much power and property. An economic system was in place where slavery played a significant part. While it was impossible to justify such a system, it was not possible to dismantle it with moral indignation and condemnation. Furthermore, the victims were still there and needed to be considered. The sugar and cotton plantations and many other profitable enterprises were in danger of collapse if slavery were abolished. Slavery is sinful; the trading in humans is immoral. This is accepted. But the facts remain. People have been enslaved. Some are still in servitude and the moral consensus regarding slavery and the legal bans enacted cannot just wipe out the sordid story.

Liberation by decree could achieve certain results but not enough. The change of heart in nations who had practised slavery and were reaping substantial rewards from the sweat of slaves needed to be expressed in practical policies. What shape should these take?

One of the first outlines of Libermann's policies we find in a letter to a very close confidant of his, Gamon, then a director of a seminary in the diocese of Clermont-Ferrand. From this letter we can see clearly that Libermann is a novice in the business of dealing with this whole question of slavery. He has no background to rely on, no real practical experience, but is convinced that there is something he can do. He writes to his friend, one senses as much to clarify his own ideas as to get some advice and encouragement:

> Our intention is to come to the aid of the black slaves or those who have been freed in the French and English colonies. These poor people are the most miserable on earth. They are totally ignorant of anything concerning religion. They have no idea of what ought to be done to be saved. Because of this ignorance, they are steeped in all kinds of vice. Many of them are not baptised, even though they belong to Christian masters. The vast majority are not married, but live together like dogs and change their women at will. The evil state of

these poor people stems from the fact that nobody is concerned about their salvation. The masters have only their own interests in mind. Even those who have been liberated are still working for masters in such conditions that differ very little from the slaves.

They work from morning to night in the burning heat and are exposed to the torrents of rain in winter. They are beaten mercilessly for the smallest mistake. They are despised by the whites and treated like animals. No other people are despised as these are; none as badly treated. For food all they have is some roots boiled with salt; cooked rice is their only bread. Once a year they might have meat. Men, women and children work without respite and with no recompense beyond the miserable nourishment they get. Just imagine people steeped in such misery without anything to console them and without hope of escape. This is something to tear asunder any sensitive Christian soul. Without any comfort, without any pleasure on earth, they inevitably get ensnared by vice and sin of all sorts. (ND. III, 76)

This tells very little about the condition of slaves at this time. It tells us quite a bit about someone who feels 'torn asunder' when he thinks of how the slaves live, eat and work. Gamon is being informed less about slave conditions than about Libermann's thinking at this time. Something has got into the mind of Libermann that is driving him to action. He sees the spiritual and material condition of slaves as truly horrible and wants to do something about it. He has scarcely anything by way of resources. The few people who are interested at this time are not very reliable. The obstacles seem to be insuperable. But something has to be done.

Libermann is regarded as one of the pioneers of the modern missionary movement. It is worth noting that 'mission' as such, does not concern him at this stage. Rather, what makes the apostolate attractive for him, as he says in this same letter, is that the people he is concerned with are 'Christians, in a country subject to the church.' France is a Christian country; the slaves in the colonies are French subjects. France has an obligation towards them. He is not reaching out to 'pagans'. He is concerned about those 'at home' who are the 'most despised and those subject to the greatest misfortune' (ND. III, 78). The fact that many of the slaves are baptised is recognised, but what is also emphasised throughout is that these people are 'despised'. The social conditions of the people contradict the status of people who are baptised into Christ. A 'Christian country, subject to the church' is not living up to its calling. This requires action.

Help was being offered. Libermann acknowledges that governments and different organisations were taking up the cause of slaves. Acknowledging this did not absolve the Christians of their obligation to do what was required of them as Christians. Governments would even help missionaries. In fact, French priests were being sponsored for the work in the colonies. This was not enough. What Libermann requires is:

> some charitable and zealous priests, filled with the Spirit of Our Lord and with his compassion for those in need and for those who are lost. Such priests should bring solace to these poor people with the tenderness and compassion of Our Lord. They should try and cultivate souls that are barren and dried up. The people are easily influenced. They are accustomed to being despised and uncared for. When they now see others coming to their assistance, people who treat them with kindness and charity, they will become fervent Christians. (ND. III, 78)

It is often remarked that one kind of slavery can be replaced by another. It is clear that neo-colonialism came hard on the heels of colonialism. The change of heart that might bring about the abolition of slavery could well be countered by a patronising attitude that would do little to give people a sense of their dignity and a way of life that would be truly theirs. In any case, the former slaving nations immediately became engaged in the 'scramble for Africa' when they outlawed slavery. The slave cargoes may not be crossing the seas, but some new form of slavery could be heading for the continent of Africa. What Libermann considered of the utmost importance was to have truly Christian people minister to the needy in such a way that they in turn would become true Christians. The Spirit of Jesus Christ is what is required above all else in those who go to help and in those who are helped.

It is worth emphasising that at the time priests were available for the colonies. However, these priests, in Libermann's estimation, were not doing the work that was required of them. Their ministry was to the colonists and not to the black slaves. So it was not just a matter of having missionaries but having a certain kind of missionary. And here a problem arose. The Holy Ghost Seminary in Paris provided priests for the colonies. This seminary had survived the French Revolution and had considerable government backing for its work. If Libermann wanted to send priests to the colonies he would have to liaise with the Superior of the Holy Ghost Seminary. This may not be easy. Only time could unravel some of the practical difficulties that might arise. For the present, there was the problem of getting territory for the few recruits. This brought about a major shift in policy.

It happened that a new dimension came to Libermann's attention at this time. Towards the end of the eighteenth century, Great Britain had settled some freed slaves in what is now Sierra Leone. America was now doing the same and repatriation to Liberia was taking place. With the slaves came Protestant missionaries. In 1833, Bishop John England of Charlestown in the United States asked *Propaganda Fide* to do something about the resettled slaves. Some religious congregations were contacted, but they did not take up the offer. The two Irish-born diocesan priests, Edward Barron and John Kelly, arrived in Monrovia in 1842. Barron left for Rome after three months to report what seemed to him a hopeless situation. The task seemed totally beyond his strength and he did not have the follow-up that would be required for the future. Back in Europe he heard of Libermann and they met. This meeting had a profound effect on Libermann and his missionary project. To help those who were considered only fit for work as slaves one had to consider the black people as such and their total environment. The concern for the slaves remains, but the main focus now is Africa. In fact, Libermann now sees that the greatest contribution he can make to the whole slave question is to contribute to the continent from which they came. Again we have him sharing his thoughts with Gamon on this issue:

> This (Africa) is the homeland of the poor blacks. These
> children of Ham are neglected everywhere, and everywhere
> they are in poverty. They go naked. Their beliefs resemble
> those of the Manicheans. And yet they are a gentle and docile
> people. (ND. IV, 63)

And with another correspondent:

> Despite the horrible state of the descendants of Ham, I have
> every reason to believe that the mission along the coast will
> produce favourable results. (ND. V. 17)

The situation of the people in Africa is viewed here from the
point of view of a Christian missionary. It is not that of an
anthropologist. It is a cry for help more than a statement of fact.
Those in need were 'Children of Ham.' Already we find the
racial issue emerging with the religious context. (The expressions
'Blacks,' 'Children of Ham,' and 'Accursed race' were used by
many authors interchangeably in the nineteenth century.) But in
the estimation of Libermann at this time, these 'Children of
Ham' were where one will find 'intelligent people and can see a
large and beautiful mission coming to be with great hopes and
with plenty of suffering and difficulties.' The 'children of Ham'
are destined to become the children of God. The mission is one
of hope even when it presents what seem to be insuperable
challenges. Hope is at the very centre of the fight against slavery
and against the prejudice against black people.

The material and social conditions of the people are of great
concern to Libermann. He did not know very much about them,
but had a general idea that these conditions were deplorable
and that something needed to be done. Above all, what was
needed was to bring to them the message of Jesus Christ. Here,
at the very beginning of his mission to Africa, he considers the
religious outlook of the Africans, and again, while his knowledge
of this is superficial and little more than could be got from
hearsay, the fact that it is taken into consideration at this stage is
quite significant. It must be remembered that he is writing to a
friend about all this and would seem to be seeking to clarify his
own ideas. He is not really trying to describe the people, their
religion, culture or material conditions. He is not in a position to
do this. Yet, if he is to reach out to help people he sees in dire

need, he must try to see them as they are in their particular environment. About their religion he has this to say:

> They believe in a Great Spirit who they say is good and benevolent towards them. They also believe in the existence of a demon, an evil spirit whom they fear greatly. They frequently offer superstitious sacrifices to this demon. This fear could help being them to accept the Christian religion. (ND. IV, 63)

The beliefs and practices of the Africans as he sees them are not so much obstacles to the people accepting Christianity as positive means for leading them to Christ. Just how fear of the demon might do this is not at all clear. It cannot be clear yet, but in the course of time it will have to be considered, as well as many other factors that are unknown for the present.

When discussing with a Superior of a convent who had shown interest in the mission to Africa and who was considering sending Sisters to the mission, Libermann gives the religion of Africans more detailed consideration. Again, his outlook is missionary and what he is seeking is a way of leading them from the known to what is as yet unknown:

> Their religion is very simple and takes a lot from Christianity. They acknowledge a Supreme Spirit who they say is good and who never causes harm. This belief would facilitate belief in the Incarnation and Redemption. They also believe in the existence of an evil spirit who is malicious, constantly bringing trouble to people, and harming them. They offer sacrifices to this demon to placate him. Here again, this will help to prepare them for belief in the central truths and prepare them for the practice of religion. (ND. IV, 17)

Liberating people from poverty and slavery will require knowledge of the social and economic conditions in which they live. Bringing the message of Christianity to them will have to take into consideration the 'seeds of the Word' that one will find and from these lead on to religious liberation. For what strikes Libermann as particularly significant in the religion of the Africans is the fear of evil spirit and the need to be on good terms with him, lest he bring evil and death on people. So the socio-religious environment has to be examined. The culture of the people has to be understood somehow if they are to be helped.

As well as the social and religious conditions, Libermann tries to get some light on the psychology of the African people. One can find him in his letters teasing out how the African views the world. The physical conditions alone will not tell the whole story; there is something that is peculiar to the psyche of the people that has to be taken into consideration. Seeking to orientate the mind of a missionary towards the mission in Guinea, he writes:

> In Guinea we will have to catechise people who are completely ignorant and who live in misery. We will have to deal with people who are extremely poor and despised. The people are uncultured, uneducated and unhygienic. However, the character of the people is gentle and docile. And this seems to be a characteristic of the black people everywhere. They are appreciative and sensitive. Their intelligence is more or less developed, depending on the country they come from. (ND. IV, 61)

The negative side of the picture of Africa and the Africans is balanced with a positive appreciation. The material conditions are portrayed in very negative terms, but the 'character' of the people is seen in a very positive light. The missionary is not to give up because of the difficulties he encounters, the poverty, the dirt, etc. What is of greatest importance are the people themselves. Goodness can be found in a people, and their material conditions must not prevent the missionary from discovering the good in people. The juxtaposition of the material poverty and the riches to be found in the character of the people can be found in so many of his letters at this time.

> Despite the horrible state of the descendants of Ham, I have reason to believe that the mission along the coast will produce great results. (ND. V, 17)

> The character of the black people is very good, kind and docile, full of respect for the priests ... The gospel will certainly be readily accepted by them. (ND. VI, 229)

If the missionary encounters conditions that he finds distasteful, he must not be discouraged. The dispositions of the people will compensate for the harshness of the environment. The greatest obstacle, it would seem, could come, not from the local people but from the foreigners. The fear of the negative influence of foreigners he shares with Gamon:

> The dispositions of the inhabitants are wonderful ... Once the truths of the faith are presented to them they accept right away, especially where the Europeans are not present. The Europeans are the major obstacle to the spread of faith, for they even persuade the local people of good will not to pay any attention to the missionaries. (ND. VI, 442)

The message of the missionary is not just one from the 'Europeans.' The message of the gospel is often opposed by the foreigners. The gospel can be at variance with the ideas and practices of many who call themselves Christian. Libermann suspected that 'Africans have great respect for European learning and are very quick to adopt European ideas' (ND. VI, 289), so he sees the danger of confusing 'European' with Christian values. In seeking the assistance of Belgians to help the African mission, he emphasises the possibilities that need to be taken into consideration and the role of religion in helping the people. What is needed, above all, is a certain quality of human relationships. This is the primary gift that the missionary can bring:

> If these poor people experience the consolation of religion to comfort them in what they endure physically and morally, their condition would not be so bad. But they have nothing. They are gentle and docile by nature. It is true that they have been known to engage in cruel behaviour, but this was from superstition or from unjust and violent provocation. In the ordinary course of life, they are good and religious people. Once instructed in the principles of the faith and worship, they remain faithful and persevere with determination. (ND. VI, 433)

Libermann sees the Africans trapped in a horrible socio-economic environment. Their religion does not help them to break through the barriers that envelop them. The Gospel message is to be their way to freedom. From without, they are despised and regarded as of little value. If they are accepted as children of God and see themselves as such, a bond is broken. If they are freed from poverty, from fear of demons, they can be free to develop as true and fervent Christians. In the Memorandum just quoted from above, we find Libermann giving a general outline of the bonds that have to be broken and the liberty that has to be achieved. Every negative characteristic has to be understood in the context of the lives of the people if it is to be corrected. The missionary must be ready to look for mitigating factors amid the most distasteful and sinful practices. The people are indolent and thieves, it is claimed. Where the necessities of life are lacking, it is no wonder that people steal, and where incentive for work is fear of being beaten, it is not surprising if people do not want to work. If sin and vice abound, that is all the more reason why help is needed to lead them to virtue. The possibilities are there; what is required is the will and determination to do something. All moral and social evils call for a response on the part of those who see these evils. The garden overgrown with weeds is one that can yield plentiful crops if cultivated. Libermann cries out for help to cultivate a large and fertile land.

The vices attributed to Africans need to be seen in the context of their whole way of life. Furthermore, they are to be seen in conjunction with the virtues of the people. Where there is a positive commitment to help, the total environment, as well as the character of the people, is examined. Libermann does not of course give a thorough and exhaustive review of the social and psychological conditions, but the fact that he takes them into consideration is of major importance. It is to be noted also that when considering the conditions of Africa, it is always in the perspective of Christian hope. The facts, no matter how bad they may seem, are seen in the light of what can be when the Christian message is accepted by the people. When the difficulties are presented in a most discouraging manner, Libermann points out that 'the problems do not arise from the character of the people but from other sources. The people are disposed to accept the Faith and to become truly religious in a way that would be hard to find elsewhere'. (ND. VI, 433) The Christian hope that comes through here is not based on solid evidence, of which there could be very little, but on the faith in the universal mission of Christ and his church.

Christian hope reaches out to distant horizons and to new possibilities. Libermann seems to have anticipated a problem that would arise in due course. Faced with what seems to be a really evil society and a people steeped in all sorts of vice, the missionary could be tempted to restrict his activity to a small group, seeking to take such a group out of the evil environment and moving into a totally new way of life. To counter the mentality that would seek to concentrate on a restricted area and a limited number, Libermann emphasises that such limitations must not be imposed. Even with the scantiest of resources and personnel, the mission must be seen in its universal dimension. This did not mean that the mission had to be seen in terms of millions of converts and of mass baptisms. Considering the whole African race, Libermann did not see the mission in terms of numbers, but in putting into place the structures that would lead the people to true freedom in Jesus Christ. When it was pointed out to him that the colonies provided more than enough scope for his mission-aries at this time, he countered:

> If we have a small corner to cultivate, we will never achieve very much. We will just vegetate and achieve nothing. I believe that the apostolic spirit consists essentially in extending the boundaries of the Church and not just in perfecting a small area. To save millions who belong to the Church for us would be wonderful, but only temporary and nothing in comparison to establishing the Faith in a pagan country. (ND. VI, 112)

Having seen first of all the conditions of the slaves and then realising that their condition was intimately connected with the people of Africa, Libermann realised that the mission was not to be seen in terms of individuals but in terms of a whole race, an entire people in need of redemption. It is worth noting here that after Libermann, the mission was seen for a time as 'cultivating a small corner.' This was done by isolating former slaves in 'Christian villages' and by concentrated efforts trying to create a

Christian elite. Experience showed that this method was flawed. The Church had to be the source of hope and freedom for the 'pagan' people as such. The Church had to take root among the people; it could not be an island surrounded by an alien environment.

In founding a missionary society, Libermann saw that the life and progress of the society had to be inspired by its sense of mission. He himself had experienced the life of the ghetto. He seemed to fear the kind of community that cut itself off from the world around it. This held for the evangelising community as well as for the community to be evangelised. The missionary society was not to be an end in itself; it had to live and prosper by the spirit that inspired its mission. When appealing to Mother Javouhey for help for his mission, Libermann makes it clear what the objective of a missionary congregation should be:

Help me, dear Sister, not to work for my own satisfaction and promote the good of the congregation under my care. God knows that this is something I reject totally with all my heart and mind – self-interest and self-aggrandisement. Help me to save the country. (ND. VI, 277)

Ideological suspicion can be a healthy antidote for those who set out to help the poor and needy. The same can be said about those who are engaged in aid projects. It is all too easy to enslave people with 'charity.' True love for people will see the potential in the people and will strive to let this develop and bear fruit. It is all too easy to be a hero among the poor and enrich oneself with the poverty of others! Missionary congregations today can take legitimate pride in their achievements. They must also, in all truth and humility, admit their shortcomings and their faults. Libermann had to admit mistakes. When his missionaries were imprudent and when their way of life led many to an early grave, he tried to analyse what might have led to this:

I do my best to follow the normal prudent course of action. I fear, however, that I may have made mistakes. I have nobody to advise me. Even those who seem to be endowed with the highest wisdom often have an egocentric perspective on issues. They readily give an opinion but fail to place themselves in the position of the one seeking advice or the particular circumstances that he is faced with. They have sets of principles that apply adequately to their own situation. Then, without any further consideration, they apply these principles where they ought to be adapted to the person and situation that is to be dealt with. (ND. VI, 192)

Inevitably, Libermann made mistakes. To move into a foreign territory, into a strange environment, was to take a risk. And in taking risks, mistakes were made. But mission demands such risk-taking. In the quotation above, it is clear that Libermann had to get advice. The advice he got was often from those with minds not at all in tune with the reality. The problems these advisors saw were totally different from the real life situation of the people that Libermann was concerned with. This kind of mindset is well illustrated in so many text books of moral theology. For many of these, the only questions that are considered are those for which a definite answer can be given and of course, is given clearly and emphatically. Moral theology, however, has to deal with the problems posed by the society; it has to take its material from the lives of people and in doing so has to deal with many grey areas. The true missionary spirit and the missionary approach to moral problems cannot rest on total security. Yet, this craving for security and for correctness plays a destructive role very often. Just to cite a common example from contemporary Africa: Canon Law is clear on the situation of Catholics who are married traditionally but who have not had a 'church' marriage. Such couples simply are not married. But if one were to move a little outside the mentality of the law, and have a good look at the life situation of people, a different conclusion might emerge, and a lot of suffering avoided.

Many find themselves in the normal 'mission' situation today. The new world brought about by the Industrial Revolution, for instance, was quite different from what went before, and so many of the working class simply found they no longer belonged to the Church. Anyone who honestly confronts contemporary issues will appreciate the dilemma of Libermann. He sought advice, and this was readily given. But then he found that the counsellors lived in a different world. Their horizons were limited to that world, and they could not envisage the real situations. Most observers of today's reality find themselves on the margin. The world of commerce, of banking, of international trade, of entertainment, of communication, of healthcare etc, is so foreign to most that to try and find solutions to the variety of issues that arise is to realise that one is peering into the unknown. To be too ready with solutions when the issues are not properly understood is to isolate oneself from the real world. Without the 'missionary' outlook, one is in danger of retreating into a ghetto and operating with a mindset that has little or no contact with the issues of contemporary society. To realise that one is dealing with a strange and new situation is no excuse for avoiding it. It is rather a challenge and a call to launch out with Christian hope (which surely excludes security) and meet people where they are.

When we see Libermann agonising over the conditions of the Africans a century and a half ago, when we find him trying to visualise the kind of people he proposed to deal with and the physical, social and moral environment that his missionaries will find themselves in, we realise how today the modern missionary must try and enter the mind of the bureaucrat, the politician, the diplomat, the stockbroker, the entertainer etc. When we see how far he was from having a true picture of Africa, we can sympathise with those who strive to find space for the gospel message in the complex society of today. We can appreciate also the frustration of so many who try to enter into the complexities of our time and come up against norms and principles that simply do not apply in present circumstances and yet are proclaimed as valid for all times. Libermann got advice and found that it missed the target. He himself was conditioned by his own milieu, culture and education, but when he tried to move out, he at least came to realise that the new world he was facing required new thinking and new policies.

To deviate from the 'safe line' is seen as imprudent. Libermann was accused of imprudence by one who was not known for being endowed with very much common sense. Confronted with the accusation of imprudence, he set about redefining the whole notion of prudence in a changing world and putting it in the context of a *modus agendi* for a mission situation. Being over-cautious is not being prudent!

I think a missionary enterprise requires prudential calculations that are at variance with what applies to conditions in our own country. Missionary conditions are quite different and belong to a different order of things. To enter such a situation requires a special Providence and exceptional grace from God. Where the work of the Church is concerned, one must rely on such a grace. This exceptional grace that is required in the mission is, in fact, to be regarded as normal for the situation. Anyone who does not rely on the exceptional grace is tempting God. If, however, Providence does not seem to provide such exceptional grace, this is no reason for despair right away. One must wait in patience and in hope. (ND. VI, 192)

The newness of the territory he was considering brought about new ways of looking at the world in general. Within the ghetto, life was simple and its problems could easily be solved. To move out was to find a different world, one which would bring new life even to the old world. It is somewhat of a cliché today to say that mission is a two-way process. The modern missionary, unlike his predecessor, does not go just to teach. He has a lot to learn. He does not go merely to make converts, but is required to be converted. This is undoubtedly true, but it may not be quite as modern as it often made out to be. Moreover, the openness towards what is different and new is often found side by side with an inability to appreciate what is of value in the old ways. Libermann got his grounding in Christianity from the Sulpicians. He appreciated this even when he found it inadequate:

The Sulpicians are holy men. They can give excellent advice on church matters. But for our work, one must not depend on them for direction. It is a known fact, that they are hardly acquainted with what happens outside their own houses. It would be quite amazing if they could understand and advise on matters that lie outside their experience. Of these they have no clear conception. (ND. VI, 118)

From the ghetto of Saverne, Libermann had entered a somewhat similar one that of St Sulpice. When he came to think of the mission to slaves, and later to the African people, he realised that St Sulpice, good as it was, did not have everything. He underwent a second conversion that was no less real than the first. Judaism gave him security for a while. He moved into a new world, the world of post-revolutionary France, and he had to change. Now another new world opens before him, and he sees the need for a change once again. This demanded courage. And courage was had at the price of suffering and being misunderstood. When the young missionaries died before they could begin their work he was accused of imprudently sending men to be slaughtered. This hurt, but it did not kill his spirit. He admits mistakes but cannot see how they could be avoided:

> Providence has been our guide. But things have not worked out the way prudence led us or even the way we feared. If we had taken the road that seemed to be the way of prudence, we would have restricted ourselves to a puny mission. In fact, it takes a big mission to attract a big crowd. (ND. VI, 191)

In the last resort, there was no easy, safe way of carrying out the mission. Mistakes were inevitable. Only by mistakes could one learn. He was reminded that the tropical climate was hazardous, and all he could say to this was to take up a mission to Africa was to expose oneself to tropical diseases. The Church does not prosper in comfortable surroundings. Of the ten missionaries who went to Africa in 1842, only two were alive a year after, and these were thought to be dead. In 1847, when another group, led by the first bishop of the society, embarked for Africa they were almost wiped out within 200 days. This was not easy to take, and yet, this is what gave courage to others to come forward and take on the challenge. Libermann faced the dilemma of abandoning the mission in order to save the lives of missionaries. It was a difficult predicament to be in. He did not want to send missionaries to their early grave. But as he put it:

> I am still committed to the work of salvation in these parts, but it has to be done in such a way as to succeed. I cannot send excellent missionaries to be butchered before they can even begin their work. (ND. VI, 372)

Semen est sanguis Christianorum. Christianity can only become a reality when it is bought at the price of bloodshed. This could not be too easily used as a rationalisation for imprudent action. It was admitted that 'the good missionaries died from excessive zeal and obedience' (ND. VI, 371). (The bishop demanded the most rigorous obedience). And again, 'the losses we incurred were, for the most part, the result of imprudence and inexperience of the climate (ND. VI, 478). Was this culpable? It is difficult to judge. 'I had no definite knowledge of the country, nor did anyone else have it.' (ND. VI, 375). But what efforts were made to find out more? He explained to his brother:

> The information I had about the coast was misleading. I looked for information from people who should have had a good knowledge of these places. I wrote to the Ministry of the Navy. All answered in writing and gave me what those who explored the coast put on record. All agreed that survival was possible if one arrived during the favourable season and took certain precautions. This was all wrong. However, there are some places that Europeans can be accustomed to. (ND. VI, 478)

With brilliant economists we can still have economic disasters. The expertise of marriage counsellors does not prevent marriage breakdown. Medicine has to cope with new diseases while it enjoys new and efficient cures. The Church, with two thousand years of experience, still has to face the unknown and the hazardous. Liberation movements will bring strife, but is that all? Ordination of women would certainly bring division, but would any benefits accompany it? The seminary system for preparing for ministry has yielded significant fruit. Would abandoning it bring about a more dynamic Christian ministry? Without actual experience, who can decide these and other contemporary issues? How can one gain the required experience without moving into the unknown?

Reflection
What inspired Libermann most of all was the vision he had formed of the African people. It was a very dark picture drawn from popular ideas of the time and from bits and pieces of information he was able to come by. Perhaps it was how the African people were seen by those who were involved in slavery and those who

would approve of the practice. Libermann's vision was not confined to the reality as he saw it; it extended to what could be and what ought to be.

Irish society has changed considerably in the last fifty years. Church organisation has not changed to the same extent. Changes have come about as reactions to decline in attendance at Mass, Confessions, shortage of priests etc. These are seen as negative trends in church life, but the opposite could be true. This needs to be explored. Jesus' example might inspire hope. Paul's 'strength in weakness' might give some encouragement.

CHAPTER FIVE

From Foreign Mission to Indigenous Church

It is relatively easy to set out on mission and to achieve some success with the grace of God. This is what every normal missionary, zealous for the glory of Jesus Christ ought to aim at. But to harness the various resources that are needed to increase, to extend and to consolidate this effort, to set up something that is solid and stable, to foresee the obstacles and take the measures necessary to overcome them, and above all, to lay a solid foundation for an apostolic venture such as Jesus Christ willed, this is indeed a very difficult task. (ND. VII, 219)

With good reason it could be said that the mission of the church *ad extra* was in many respects carried out as extending the church at home to 'our beloved subjects in foreign parts'. The missionary church in practice was following the imperial expansion of the world powers of the day. If a territory was conquered or fell under the influence of some European power it would require assistance to have the kind of ecclesiastical organisation that the mother country enjoyed. Such a system could be brought about by the 'ordinary missionary, zealous for the glory of God'. To have something 'solid and stable' it would need to have the customs and structures of the colonising power. However, Libermann saw that 'to lay a foundation for an apostolic venture such as Jesus Christ willed' required something quite different.

Libermann was aware that, in the case of Africa, it would be possible for zealous missionaries to achieve considerable and praiseworthy results. He realised too, that there could be a certain danger in this. From the start, his concern was to 'lay a solid foundation,' and this was recognised to be a much more difficult task than getting enthusiastic people performing heroic deeds. And just as the Second Vatican Council was not merely concerned with individuals to be saved, but whole cultures to be evangelised or re-evangelised, so the challenge was to plant the seeds of the gospel where they could take root and flourish.

Such action needs to be carefully planned, officially approved and energetically encouraged by the central organs of church administration. From his first encounter with *Propaganda Fide* in Rome, six years earlier, he seemed to get the impression that more conviction and determination were required at headquarters. Fr Barron, who had lived in Rome and knew the Roman scene, kept up contacts with *Propaganda Fide*. He was named Prefect Apostolic of The Two Guineas and Sierra Leone where Britain had some repatriated former slaves. Soon after, he was named Vicar Apostolic of a vast Vicariate from the Senegal River in the north to the Orange River in the south, a total of about 5,000 miles long with no limits in the interior. He was looking for help and he met Libermann who promised seven missionaries.

This band of missionaries left for Africa in September 1843. They joined Fr Kelly in Cape Palmas in November. Bishop Barron was still in Europe and did not arrive in Africa until January 1844. By then a number of the missionaries had died, and Fr Kelly had left the mission and returned to America. It was not clear to the missionaries where they were supposed to be. Libermann had appointed them to one area and the Vicar Apostolic to another. Most of the missionaries were dead within six months of arriving. A priest and a brother had survived but no news from them reached Libermann and it was thought that all were dead.

The deaths of most of the missionaries and the lack of proper organisation discouraged Bishop Barron and he left for Europe to hand in his resignation to *Propaganda Fide* and return to pastoral work in America.[1] The vast Vicariate was without a Vicar and missionaries.

Libermann was devastated by what had happened. He was accused of sending men to certain death. He had the support of the members of his congregation. To Le Vavasseur he wrote:

---

1. The mission of Barron has been described in great detail by Seán P. Farragher C.S.Sp., *Edward Barron, Unsung Hero of the Mission to Africa*, Paraclete Press, Dublin, 2004.

You must have got my letter telling of the disaster in Guinea. That news, far from discouraging the brothers here has strengthened their determination to sacrifice themselves for the salvation of Guinea. Seven are ready for appointments and six of these have volunteered for Guinea. They are tormenting me to let them go. But the mission is not for missionaries to die, but for the salvation of souls. It is absolutely impossible to save the country unless we have an indigenous clergy.' (ND. VI, 419)

Libermann was not for quitting despite the loss of life of his men. He was concerned about the effect of Bishop Barron's resignation might have in Rome and the future of the new Vicariate. He wrote a memorandum to *Propaganda* announcing the deaths and proposing a 'Project for the salvation of the people in the coast of Africa.' (ND. VI, 391-394) While mourning the loss of his missionaries he still had to keep in mind the millions who were in darkness and ready to embrace the light of truth. The kernel of his project was to have a centre in a suitable place in Africa where young men would get some training before sending them to a seminary in Rome. At the time he thought Europeans could not survive in the African climate and so African priests were absolutely necessary. The following year an Instruction, *Neminem Profecto*, on the indigenous clergy in mission countries, was published by *Propaganda*. In the meantime the proposal for training young Africans in Rome was shelved and a more elaborate Memorandum was prepared,

In August 1846, Libermann addressed this Memorandum to the Cardinal Prefect of *Propaganda Fide*.[2] This Memorandum must surely be regarded as fundamental to an understanding of his missiology. Surprisingly, it has not been given serious consideration by students of Libermann until more recent times.[3] Basically, the Memorandum is a plea to Rome to consider the policies and the procedures that ought to be operational in promoting

---

2. This is found in ND. VIII, 222-277. Most references in this chapter refer to this and reference will be indicated simply by the page number.
3. In the mid 1970s the major study I could find was a doctoral thesis by Jos Kirkels in the University of Strasbourg in 1972. (unpublished). Since then enormous work has been done by Paul Coulon, in *Libermann*, Cerf, 1988 and in other publications of his.

the African mission. The literary style of the Memorandum has little to recommend it. The fact that it is written by someone who had never been to Africa becomes quite apparent. Knowledge of conditions in Africa has been gleaned from various sources, few of them of any real value. The value of the Memorandum lies in that it comes from someone who is absolutely convinced that the church has a serious obligation towards the African people and the whole continent. Action ought to be taken as a matter of urgency.

This sad episode, the deaths of the missionaries (two survived, though Libermann thought they had died) and the apparent failure of the American initiative, placed Libermann in a very difficult position. His community was determined to carry on with the mission and so he decided not to give up but to press on. Rome had now established a Vicariate so the mission would no longer be to the trading posts on the West Coast of Africa but to the Continent and its people.

Libermann negotiated with the Director of the French Colonies, Galos, for the missionaries to be supported and financed. This brought some encouragement and finance for Libermann's men, something that Barron sadly lacked. In negotiations with Rome he got one of the pioneers, Tisserant, appointed Prefect Apostolic of the Two Guineas but he died *en route* to his mission in a shipwreck in December 1845. Missionaries were still being sent to Africa in the meantime in close collaboration with the Director of the Colonies. Pope Gregory XVI died in June 1846 and Pius IX was elected pope that same month. Libermann went to Rome in July and presented the famous Memorandum to *Propaganda Fide* on August 1846. Later that year one of Libermann's missionaries, Truffet, was appointed Vicar Apostolic of the Two Guineas.

The American venture would have shown the wisdom of Libermann's insistence on a community for the Africa mission. The admirable zeal of Barron and Kelly was not enough to sustain their project. Likewise the deaths of the early missionaries could have destroyed the whole initiative were it not for the continuity that was given by the community supporting the mission. From a position of now being *de facto* charged with the Vicariate of the Two Guineas, Libermann drew up the Memorandum. As we shall see the emphasis is not at all on control of territory but on people in need of help.

The opening paragraph sets the tone. The time has come to act:

> When we look at the condition of black people anywhere in the world today, we may be tempted to think that they are cursed by God from the outset and oppressed beneath a burden of ignorance and suffering. Everywhere, they are in a truly miserable condition of ignorance and superstition. Nobody stretches out a hand to free them from the infernal power that holds them in bondage ... And yet, they are made in the image of God like all other people, and they are ready to welcome the gift of faith that they have never known. (223)

Here we see Libermann pleading to Rome to look out to the continent of Africa, to consider the condition of people there, and then to see what ought to be done. A glance will reveal people in suffering, in distress and neglected by the world. More than a century later, the church did take an outward look in trying to recognise what was happening in the world. 'The joy and hope, the grief and anguish of people of our time, especially of those who are poor or afflicted in any way' was of major concern to Vatican II. More than a century earlier, the plea was made that those who seem to be accursed by God, who are regarded as the wretched of the earth, ought to be seen as children of God, people made in the image of God and destined for eternal life. Africa is not a Dark Continent; it is part of God's creation. The simple theological truth that black people are equal in dignity to any other human beings on earth is a call to change many of the common prejudices concerning them. This is the first step because, as Libermann puts it, it is commonly believed that:

> These people will never be able to look after themselves, nor persevere in what one might try to inculcate in them. They are stupid, incompetent, heartless, thieves, incorrigible, corrupt and evil by nature, and so it is useless to try and do anything for them. But we cannot believe that so many people could be excluded in God's wisdom from the immense benefits of the Redemption. (225-226)

No matter how bad the situation of Africa may seem, let it be painted in the darkest of colours, let it be considered in its worst light, and all this will point to the need for action. Whatever be the actual condition of the people, one thing is quite clear: they are not excluded from sharing in the Resurrection of Jesus Christ. No amount of research can show that human beings are not children of God, redeemed by the blood of Christ. Again, the theology is simple and down-to-earth, and yet it has tremendous force if accepted as true. Then, to show that often the 'children of this world are wiser than the children of light,' another aspect of what is happening in the present-day world is highlighted:

> We see all over Europe that there has arisen a spontaneous movement to come to the aid of the black race and bring them out of their misery. We see many societies, commercial as well as humanitarian, actively engaged in this way. We see the most powerful governments of Europe employing considerable resources in bringing civilisation to them. (224)

'The signs of the times' have theological importance. If the secular world is showing interest in Africa it cannot be simply because Africa is in total darkness and entirely useless. The church needs to see what is happening and not be left tied to the past. How does Libermann view the nascent 'scramble for Africa?' His view on this matter is of fundamental importance for an understanding of his mission as a whole:

> We see these events as the work of God who, having left the people for so long in darkness and suffering, now sets events in motion to bring them from the misery that afflicts them. These trends that can bring happiness could also bring dangers with them ... Many Europeans of ill-repute and many enemies of the church have infiltrated the movements and this can only bring disaster to the souls of the people. (224)

Europe is getting a new interest in Africa. This is a fact and one that has positive potential. It ought not to be ignored. What is happening in the world has to be taken into account. One must see the reality and form a judgement on what is taking place. Much of what is going on is for the good and must be appreciated. The dangers need to be taken into account too, and from an assessment of the perils comes a challenge for the church. The interest in Africa is part of the 'Fatherly Providence of God' and within the scheme of things the church is called 'to take a stand and bring the light of faith and the grace of salvation to bear on these movements that aim at bringing material benefits'. (225)

The European interest in Africa raised many questions. But the reality of that interest and the possible consequences for Africa had to be taken into account if one were to strive to establish something solid and truly beneficial for the people of Africa. Later, we shall take a look at the notion of 'civilisation' that Europeans would bring. For the present, Libermann wants Roman authorities to be aware of the movement towards Africa, and to make policies and develop strategies accordingly. But this was not an easy matter. Something new was happening, and the best one could hope for was to be in on the act, as it were, and from practical involvement try to bring the gospel message to people. This work had to be co-ordinated and promoted by Rome. That is why, before beginning at all, he sought Roman approval, 'in order to know the will of God and whether the plan of action was the right one.' The proposal was examined and 'the Cardinal encouraged us to do everything possible to persevere in our vocation'. (ND. III, 78)

Still, four years later Libermann could complain:

> We are in a state of doubt all this time. We are not sure what plans God has for us. The Holy See has never spoken in a positive manner about the mission that we want to undertake. The Cardinal Prefect merely assented to what we proposed. So, not having any assurance of God's will, we have to be guided by events and by Providence. Prudence requires that we be flexible in God's hands. (ND. VI, 488)

Libermann's first mission was to be to the French colonies, and in particular, to the slaves in the colonies. He had considered some of the difficulties this mission would encounter from the white population. Writing about the situation in the colonies and perhaps aware that Africa could one day have a similar problem, Libermann warns newly appointed bishops of the danger to the church of such a situation:

The white people own almost all the land. Before the emancipation of the slaves, the whites were *de jure* and *de facto* rulers of the colonies. They are the *de facto* rulers at present and are likely to remain in this position for some time to come. Their absolute power over the slaves and the privileges of class that they enjoy are the source of all sorts of evil. The white man considers himself to be infinitely superior by nature to the lower creatures around him. These he regards as having been created to serve him, to provide for his happiness and to increase his fortune, to give him pleasure and satisfy his whim. (ND. XII, 246)

The basic theological principle has to have practical application. All people are children of God; all are redeemed by Jesus Christ. Whatever be the accepted way of life in the colonies, this basic tenet has to be adhered to. If some are in a position of superiority over others, this has to be corrected. It may not be easy, and there are sure to be many objections.

But, it could be objected that the people are not really in a condition to be evangelised. Their whole way of life, their level of intelligence, their morals would make it impossible for them to be converted to Christianity. Experiences in India and China in the past had revealed a certain degree of ethnocentricity in the mentality of church leaders. Unless there was a change of mentality, the same problem could arise in Africa. Again, some very basic, simple truths are proposed whereby the work of evangelisation should be undertaken:

The people need to be taught in a simple manner and in their own language. The total lack of formal education would make it impossible for them to grasp a technical presentation. But the basic truths can be understood thoroughly ... Many black people would be able to compete for a prize in catechism in Paris, not of course, in their manner of expression but as regards the basic knowledge of the topic. (227)

In clear simple language, Libermann contends that the mission requires that a distinction be made between the truths of the faith and the way in which these truths are expressed. Orthodoxy in matters of Catholic doctrine could be seen in terms of semantics. Shortly before Vatican II, a strongly worded instruction from Rome required seminarians to be taught philosophy and theology in Latin. Primary school children often had to learn answers of a catechism that were totally incomprehensible to the children. But 'orthodoxy' was important; understanding didn't matter, it would seem. An African who had no formal education whatsoever could grasp the truths of Christianity just as well as any European. This fact had to be recognised as a basic principle for evangelisation in the continent. Doctrine that had become fossilised in technical formula had to be unearthed, and presented in the language of the people and according to the culture of the people. This is simply a matter of common sense, of course, but it needed to be said and still needs to be emphasised. Much of the debate about inculturation, after all, is simply an application of the above quotation.

A very important point in this regard is to recognise that presenting the doctrine of Christ in simple language is not just making allowances for stupid or illiterate people. Often this impression is given when inculturation is in question. Rarely does one hear of the need for inculturation in the modern technological world. It is usually considered in connection with the so-called developing world. But if the truths of the faith are to be presented in any culture, then the way such truths are expressed will depend on the particular culture. Libermann did not want *Propaganda* to make allowances for a backward people. He insisted:

> There are some among them with a high degree of intelligence that is above the ordinary. We need not, then, be troubled by the notion of missionaries constantly caring for them. Missionaries assure us that there are many with minds that are sharp and open and capable of development ... A black person who was a slave, who could not read or write or do arithmetic, was found to be an excellent mechanic. About thirty slaves formed a party to fight for their freedom and worked out their plans so well as to escape detection. In a period of six hours they had organised several thousands of their fellows. This shows that among the black people there are those who have intelligence and commitment ... In America quite a few emancipated have become quite well-off. (228)

This sounds almost banal. But Libermann was convinced that Africans are not lacking in intelligence – academic or emotional. Yet, there are still people who think that foreign experts are required to make plans for the development of Africa without taking into account the skills and the knowledge of the local people. It is unfortunate that many consider Western education necessary for Africa. Western society is notoriously wasteful in the use of natural and human resources and yet would teach poor people how to make 'progress' when these people can prosper without the expenditure of enormous energy supplies, destruction of the environment, and high unemployment.

What of the moral condition of Africans? Are their morals so bad as to render evangelisation impossible? Is it not true that the people are inveterate thieves, incurably lazy, and sexually incorrigible? The church is in constant danger of forgetting that Jesus came, not for the just, but for sinners. He befriended the tax-collectors and prostitutes, for they too were children of God. Now, as we have noted in the previous chapter, the Africans were seen to lack moral values. This of course is not a reason for inaction. But one must understand the situation. Take the accusation, for instance, about stealing. This is how Libermann saw it:

> The tendency to steal is a result of the stage of development of the people. The different things the Europeans bring are a source of curiosity for them that we cannot understand in our ways of thinking. Europeans seem to them to be of a different nature altogether. It is only natural that they are captivated by a desire to possess what the European has ... But when they are instructed and educated, when they are taught the principles of the faith and taught to appreciate the things that the Europeans bring, when, moreover, they come to understand that Europeans are their brothers, that they are all children of the same God, when they are taught to love and serve God, then it will be seen that the people will change their behaviour. (231-232)

As this was being written, another Jew, Karl Marx, was preoccupied with the social conditions in Europe. Was it right that so few could possess so much while so many lacked the necessities of life? Had the poor and dispossessed a right to what they needed? I do not propose to answer such questions here, but anyone who is mission-minded, who is prepared to consider the condition of the poor, the hungry and the unemployed, must question many accepted moral positions. In a simple down-to-earth way, Libermann does this. It is seen as morally and socially reprehensible for someone to steal from another. But when a 'development agency' spends millions on some project, it is normally not seen as stealing if some foreign workers get inordinately high salaries, live in luxury, and do little in return. It is generally admitted that this is the case, for instance, with many United Nations projects. The United States, for instance, is very critical of corruption in Africa and with reason. Corruption is rampant. But it will not consider dealing in arms as being morally wrong. Today we need to take a common-sense look at many practices that are considered normal and part of the world of current business and trade in the light of the gospel and not merely in the light of contemporary culture. This matter comes up again in another Memorandum already referred to:

> The black people are thieves and liars. When they were in slavery, they were such and could not be otherwise. But the thieving and lying was no worse than is the case of the white people. The slaves and their families were kept in cruel captivity. They lived in misery, malnourished, badly housed and clothed. They had no way of alleviating these persistent privations. At the same time they saw their masters living in luxury. They saw slavery as an injustice. They believed they had a right to some recompense whenever this could be got. And despite all, people appear to be astonished by the frequency of robbery ... When the masters treat them properly and feed them adequately, they may have little reason to complain about robbery. (ND. XII, 253)

Could this be seen as Marxism?
Africa could be a happy hunting ground for the 'Seven Deadly Sins.' There they could be found in abundance! Could the sin of sloth be eradicated? *Propaganda Fide* was asked to consider the following scenario:

The people are forced by being beaten and by ill-treatment to work like animals. They get no respite and gain nothing from their efforts. From infancy they are brought up with a horror of work. Is it surprising, then, that they hate work and despise all sorts of work done by slaves? Work and slavery are synonymous. So too are idleness and freedom. But when they are liberated from the burdens laid upon them, when someone takes an interest in them and teaches them to be good Christians, then they might work much more diligently than the Europeans do under the tropical sun. (234)

'Why see the speck in your brother's eye and not the log in your own?' Jesus once asked. The idle rich have ample time to see those who waste time doing little or nothing! They often conclude from such prolonged observation that poverty is the result of laziness.

Inevitably, the question of sexual immorality would arise. That such exists is admitted. There follows then what could appear to be an application of situational ethics. To begin with, it is claimed that 'to understand people, they must not be judged in exceptional circumstances regarding these as normal'. (252) The total context of their lives needs to be taken into account if one is to understand the nature of the evil:

The people are born in frightful misery, left without help, humiliated, debased, treated like brutes with strong passions in a climate that intensifies the passions. And then there are sensible people who still expect their corruption should evoke amazement and discouragement. (229)

Finally, what has to be kept in mind is the hope 'that once Christianity takes root among the African people, abuses will gradually be overcome'. (239) What is required is a mission that will take stock of the situation and strive to bring about some improvement. To be aware of the difficulties that exist is not a reason for discouragement, but rather a challenge to do something to improve the situation:

The faults we have noticed among the black people as being common among them, are a certain weakness of character, a temperament that tends to indolence which seems to be common in the tropics, a tendency to vanity and over-sensitivity which required that they be treated with moderation, kindness and encouragement. (236)

As we have seen, Libermann had foreseen the involvement of Europeans in Africa. He also had some knowledge of the situation in the colonies where slavery was being practised. From the start, he was anxious to provide a different kind of ministry for the colonies than what was in place. To this end he was able to get three bishops appointed to three French colonies. In this way, he hoped to sow the seeds of an indigenous church. In writing to these bishops he warned against the dangers of racism, something that had entered into the life of the colonies. Racism was part and parcel of life in the colonies. Very few escaped from it. Still, he noted:

There are some wonderful examples of people who resisted despite all. They often had to pay dearly and were objects of persecution. The resistance was as heroic as it was rare ... The Voltarian education sowed the seeds of unbelief in their hearts and took from them the only means they had of restraining their violence and their passions. And there are those also who have neither land nor money nor slaves but take pride in the prerogatives of their race and the vices that go with it. (ND. XII, 247)

While trying to get *Propaganda Fide* more involved in form-ulating mission policy, Libermann was trying also to get the French Government actively involved. He informed a govern-ment minister of his plans for the colonies and for Africa:

I wish to propose to Your Excellency the plan we have adopted from the beginning for the religious instruction and the civilisation of the African people and the means we wish to adopt to carry out this plan. The general plan is to send out European missionaries; to form an indigenous clergy and to set up schools to teach agriculture, arts and crafts. (ND. VI, 284)

Co-operation with the government was seen to be possible and desirable. But Libermann was aware of the dangers. As ever, risks were part of a missionary apostolate, and the greatest danger might be not to take any risk at all and leave things as they were. To a community in Africa that had come into conflict with some French officials, he wrote:

> The French Government will help us because it is in its own interest to do so. I'm convinced that something can be achieved in this way for the salvation of souls ... I know that circumstances can arise when politics will be in opposition to what we want, but what of that? It is better to give way at times than to lose the opportunity. In fact, other missions are helped by the government. (ND. VI, 281)

What is interesting in this regard is that Libermann seems to have got more co-operation from government authorities than from Rome. Of course, to get this he had to set out his programme in such a way as to get the help he needed and, at the same time, not compromise his mission. In his diplomatic efforts he had one guiding principle – the welfare of the Africans. He once explained to his friend and collaborator, Mother Javouhey:

> The Ministry (of the Navy) has asked us to work for the civilisation of these areas. It is willing to help us in whatever way it can to establish the faith. It is true that in such circumstances the interests of religion and of the state are the same and require the same programme of action. We must combine our efforts with those of the temporal powers, work in harmony, and we can be assured of achieving something of value for the poor people of Africa. (ND. VI, 274)

How could governments be instruments of evangelisation? Helping the poor and the oppressed was the work of evangelisation, and anyone can participate in this. In the 1840s, it must be remembered that the Holy See was a 'temporal power' and was not at all anxious to give up its power at a time when such power was under siege. Governments too, can be instruments in evangelisation – in bringing Good News to the poor and the needy.

Rome had a significant role to play in setting out policies and procedures for the African mission. By creating the Vicariate of the Two Guineas it had changed the focus of the missionary fields of apostolate. This had been restricted almost entirely to providing priests for the trading posts along the coast – a ministry that could be seen by Africans as part of the business of slavery and intimately connected with the corruption and brutality of the trading in humans. With the failure of the mission to Congo, the interior of the continent had been practically abandoned.

The very short time Barron and Kelly spent in Africa showed a glaring defect in mission planning. Rome could appoint a Vicar Apostolic, grant him powers, many of which were irrelevant to the work at hand, but *Propaganda Fide* did not have the means, financial or in personnel to follow up by making the newly formed Vicariate a reality in ecclesiastical terms. Gregory XVI had spent enormous sums in trying to pacify the Papal States at home and Bishop Barron could not depend on Rome to provide much assistance. Libermann, on the other hand, had been able to attract quite a few men for the African mission and also to get considerable financial help for their mission. Barron's appeal to the British government got little more than the vague promises of protection that the Crown affords to any of its citizens.

In the attempt to put the missionary project on a solid foundation, Libermann held most of the trump cards in having the personnel and the finance. What was needed then was a general plan for the project. This had to be concerned first of all with the people to be evangelised. If these were seen by missionaries or by Rome in the manner of some Jewish elements in the early church regarded the Gentiles, as not fit material for evangelisation, then the whole project could not succeed. The church *vis-à-vis* the African people had to adopt a view that was contrary to that generally accepted at the time. The fact that the African people were in no way inferior in dignity to any others on earth had to be accepted in practice. The church to be propagated in Africa ought to be a church in which all are equal as children of God. An important structural element in this church had to provide evidence for this equality. Leadership had to be seen as coming from the native people and not from abroad.

Reflection

By the year 1846 Libermann's mission field had developed significantly. Hitherto he had concentrated on a mission to the slaves in the colonies. Now his attention is focused on the continent of Africa. Initiatives at repatriation of Africans from the United States to Liberia and Sierra Leone and contact with Bishop Barron helped to bring about the interest in Africa but the more he reflected on the condition of the slaves the more he realised the importance of the whole continent.

With his friend, Luquet, in Rome he brought a renewed strategy to the Pope. The major concern now was to promote the development of the African people. For this to be achieved the Africans themselves would have to be missionaries to themselves eventually. Foreign missionaries might plant the seed but the harvesting would be done by the local people. From the beginning the basic structures had to be established to train leaders for the various tasks to promote integral development.

In efforts to bring a mission to Europe, obstacles are inevitable. The memory of the power and prestige of the past will discourage the tiny efforts being made for renewal of the church. An 'indigenous' ministry will seem to fall short of standards set by seminaries. If the Good News is to be rooted in the soil of contemporary culture it will seem that the gospel message is being diluted. How the Holy Spirit might work cannot be foreseen. To what extent Western culture is open to receive the message of Christ needs to be tested in a spirit of faith, hope and love.

CHAPTER SIX

Mission and Church: Basic structures

> It is not enough to set out on mission with the general intention of converting the infidel. Right from the start, we must have a more definite and a more positive and more focused aim. To achieve our objective, we must put in place right from the beginning what is required for the effective implantation of our religion in the soil. For this, what is required is a strong hierarchical organisation. (ND. VII, 242)

In the last chapter, it was shown how Libermann looked for direction from Rome for his mission. It was noted that he got little that would help him from *Propaganda* to guide his first steps and had to rely on his own resources. From the start, however, he had some very definite ideas about what was needed. Mission meant moving into the unknown, so there would always be an unknown factor in the mission equation. But if the territory of the mission was necessarily obscure, the starting point had to be definite and clear. The mission was the work of the church. The 'general intention of converting pagans' may sometimes have been portrayed as the aim of the zealous missionary in the popular imagination. But this was not enough, nor was it the correct response to a missionary vocation.

The church must have a mission policy. For Libermann 'the effective implantation of our religion in the soil' was the aim of mission. The environment, the soil, would be new, and so the planting would have to take account of this. The missionary must not just move on aimlessly. He must know that he has to lay a foundation for others to build on. The foundation had to be properly prepared. The church would have to take root in a new territory. The focus then had to be on building on the alien land a structure that would endure.

The history of the church had provided the general plan for the structure. Libermann's fundamental strategy for the missionary was to form an indigenous ministry. From the outset the missionaries had to be convinced on the necessity of forming a local clergy that would be drawn from a Christian community. Community was of major importance in the building of the new church. The mission had to begin with community and continue by building community. The church as community dictated the kind of foundation that was required in the missionary work, no matter where the mission operated.

When he went to Rome in 1840, Libermann wrote a short Memorandum to *Propaganda*. In this he tried to justify the request he was making for founding a society for the evangelisation of the black people. The primary reason for founding a new congregation was set out in this Memorandum:

> If we live in community we might be able to form an indigenous clergy in the countries to which we will be sent. This seems to us to be of primary importance and absolutely necessary to remedy the evils of these poor countries. (ND. II, 71)

The work was not that of individual pioneers but of a community that would provide stability and continuity. So strong was his conviction regarding the need for community that he immediately set about composing a rule for it. This was at a time when he did not have much hope of getting permission for the society. The rule required working out clearly what the society should aim at. He laid down that the members of the congregation, 'when they settle in a country they must do everything in their power to establish an indigenous clergy there.' (ND. II, 253) For this the missionaries should set up the necessary structures to train suitable candidates for the priesthood.

The ministry for the colonies had developed along the lines of the civil administration. The clergy would be recruited in the home country and sent to produce abroad a replica of the home church. This was not acceptable for Libermann. The church could not be a colonial imposition. The Incarnate Word had to take flesh, as it were, in the new soil. Jesus must not be an alien to people. He must be one of them. When the main focus of mission changed to Africa the need for a local clergy became clearer. It was made clear to Bishop Barron what the young society was all about:

> I must now share with you something that I have been thinking of for some time and which has been one of my major preoccupations: it is to set up a place in France for the education of young blacks. If we succeed in this, the youth who may not have the qualities required for priesthood, will be taught some trades. These trades will be very useful for their fellow countrymen. Those who are suitable will be encouraged to go on to the priesthood. I believe that we must absolutely have an indigenous clergy. Once we have a few, others will be attracted and will follow. (ND. VI, 53)

The foundation for the new church in Africa would be the African people. The people would need to be educated in different disciplines; and from among those some would be priests, but all would be in some way or other apostles of Jesus. It was not just a case of having a seminary for formation of the clergy in France. The 'seminary' in Libermann's view was inclusive and would be required to educate for the variety of ministries required by the people. It would seem that very few clergy shared Libermann's ideas in this regard. In letters to his priest friends, we find very little. Interestingly, we find him sharing his ideas with lay people.

In order to find out more about conditions in the colonies and in Africa, Libermann made contact with a certain Isaac Louverture, a Haitian by birth, the son of the renowned freedom fighter, Toussaint Louverture. Toussaint was involved in the struggle for an independent Haiti. He was exiled to France in 1802 and died there the following year in prison, a year before Haiti became independent. Isaac lived in France, and Libermann contacted him, seeking information about the colonies and about Africa. He tells Louverture of his plan 'to set up a seminary as soon as possible and form an indigenous clergy so that Haiti will be able to do without foreigners'. (ND. VI, 63) This is significant, because Haiti had become independent from France in 1804. We shall have some more to say about Haiti later. For the present, what is being highlighted is conversation with the descendant of a former slave and freedom fighter. In this

Libermann admits his lack of knowledge of Africa and its people but affirms his plan to:

> set up several houses for the education of young Africans ... In the beginning, they will be given basic knowledge that is required of any person in the ordinary course of life: reading, writing, arithmetic, etc, and with these, elements of moral and religious education ... Some will be selected for further studies, and others will be trained in trades and crafts according to their abilities and aptitudes ... So that this plan be successful there ought to be uniformity in the education of the different classes. The knowledge of the lay person ought to be of the same standard as that of the clergy. The education ought to have the same objective as well: to enlighten people and strengthen them in virtue and in religion. The only difference between the two classes is that one will spread sacred, the other profane knowledge. Furthermore, those who are to bring civilisation to Africa should have the same mind and the same objectives and live by the same principles as those who are to promote morals and learning. Otherwise, one will destroy what others build. (ND. VI, 65-66)

The mission of the church must never be a kind of ecclesiastical colonialism. The programme Libermann had for Africa would try and ensure that Africans would, in the words of Pope Paul VI, be 'missionaries to themselves' as soon as possible. However, in the mid-nineteenth century, this may have been an idea with very little popular appeal in ecclesiastical circles. It is interesting to note that the most detailed outline of the plan for evangelisation by establishing a local church leadership is outlined to a layman who would be expected to have close sympathies with the local population. The mission policy was one of unity in diversity. A wide diversity of ministries was required but a unity of outlook was needed to bring stability and harmony to a people.

It is not only the idea of an indigenous clergy proposed here that is striking, but also the kind of clergy. In this one notices the missionary dimension coming through. The clergy are to be trained, not in some clerical institution, but in one where others are being trained also. The mission outlook sees the need for a diversified ministry. Education in agriculture, in trades, as well as academic education is all part of a programme of evangelisation. This seems natural in the context of helping people, ministering to the needs of people in their life-situation.

Much has been said and written on the question of an indigenous clergy. Today, one might think that this problem is solved in Africa. The seminaries are full, more are being built, convents are being extended, and congregations that are dying out in Europe are recruiting in Africa. Missionary societies have been in place for some time and are sending missionary priests and sisters to countries around the world. This is an interesting development that is taking place, no doubt. But so much of what is happening goes counter to the missionary idea of an indigenous ministry. The seminaries are mere copies of structures that are outdated in today's world. 'Africanisation' is little more than replacing whites with blacks and keeping the foreign structures and institutions intact. Of course, in time, Africa will produce its own form of ministry, but this must not be seen as a dark copy of what once flourished in Europe. Africanisation is not mere translation. Not everything imported from abroad will be adapted to the African climate and the African soil. The advocates of African priests to minister in Europe often assume that what the European churches need is simply men to fill the vacancies left by the dwindling clergy there. The 'reverse' mission is not the answer. Europe needs more than just a post-Reformation clergy, and it would be wrong to expect Africa to provide such an outmoded kind of ministry in today's world.

Libermann tried to propagate the idea of an indigenous ministry in Rome also. Even before the Memorandum of 1846, he wrote a long letter to the Cardinal Prefect in November 1844 in which he proposes training programmes similar to the one above. There are subtle nuances in the letter to Rome. The priority would seem to be the religious instruction of the youth. 'Those of greatest piety and ability will be chosen for further studies and will be advanced to the priesthood. Others will be taught agriculture and trades.' All will help to spread the faith. The catechists in this proposal are not a group apart. They are those who have got a technical or academic training. 'Those who have learned agriculture or trades will be of great assistance to their African priests to spread the Catholic faith.' (ND. VI, 391-399) The clerical dimension is given priority here, but still, the vision is inclusive of other ministries.

Early on, Libermann had the idea that the school for African children should be in France. Soon he changed his mind. To the Cardinal Prefect he suggested that Rome should provide the most suitable site for the formation of the future ministers. He thought that the ideal setting would be 'under the eyes of the Vicar of Jesus Christ who is responsible for the whole church.' Furthermore, there could be problems with having the school in any other country 'because if it is in a particular country, anyone who does not belong to that country might be excluded'. (ND. VI, 395) One can sense some hesitation about having the institution for Africans outside of Africa as it could mean domination by a particular country. Rome was considered as being somehow 'neutral' and universal and open to all people. But this idea too was changed, and his final option was for the education of Africans to be in Africa.

If Libermann was wary about education of Africans being dominated by a particular country, he was concerned that education should be seen in as broad a perspective as possible. The 'seminary' was not to be an enclosed clerical institution. It had to cater for the needs of the people and, therefore, must not be just for the formation of clergy. The ministry had to be seen in its widest sense and not just in clerical terms. The carpenters and mechanics would have a part in the ministry of spreading the Good News just as well as the priests, each category in its own way. Perhaps the experience of the ghetto of Saverne, where he was trained for Jewish ministry but found that he had been cut off from the mainstream of life in France at the time, gave him insight into the kind of ministry that was required in a changing world. Africans were children of God and citizens of the world. They had to take their rightful place in the world.

With regard to the ministry as such, Libermann wished its scope to be extended. For this he put forward the following proposal to *Propaganda* for consideration which shows how he was anxious to break with the then practice but to take up a tradition that had been neglected for centuries:

Your Eminence, we propose for your approval something that may have been discontinued in other missions, but which could have beneficial results in ours, that is to allow bishops to confer on catechists Tonsure and Minor Orders even though they are not destined for the priesthood. We ask that these be allowed to wear ecclesiastical dress in the church during services. These men would thereby be greatly encouraged in their duty to work for the spiritual well-being of their fellow countrymen ... and they could also replace the priests to some extent, presiding over congregations of the faithful in public prayer services. (246-247)

This proposal was put to the Sacred Congregation and the response was simply 'Negative'. The summary that was proposed for consideration was not quite the one suggested by Libermann, in that it specifically mentioned that those in minor orders would not be obliged to celibacy. This was not what Libermann had asked for. It would seem that the carpenter, the mason, the mechanic could be admitted into a ministry officially recognised by the church. At this time the Minor Orders had become obsolete and had little or no meaning outside the clerical establishment. The proposal to *Propaganda* at least should have raised the question of the value of the institution of Minor Orders in the life of the church. The mission could open up such a discussion; a new initiative might open up new possibilities for evangelisation. It could lead also to the abolition of what had become obsolete and irrelevant in ecclesiastical practice. This was something that those who were not mission-minded would fear most of all, for mission requires not only moving into a new world, but also abandoning one's security at home.

What applies to mission is often regarded as being somewhat exotic, remote and experimental. This ought not to be the case. Mission is part of the normal activity of the church as it reaches out to the changing world. When the church or a particular church in any area is incapable of change, then it is in danger of death. When Libermann began to consider the African mission, he became aware of the home situation in a much clearer way and saw the need for new thinking. It is all very well to propose

an indigenous clergy for Africa. In any case, there were serious
doubts then about the possibility of Europeans surviving in that
continent, particularly in the interior. It was not only considerations
of climate that dictated the need for indigenous ministries.

The very constitution of the church as Catholic required this.
The fundamental issue with regard to the indigenisation of the
church is not merely a matter of race or colour, but of an
appropriate ministry. One might have local clergy who are
uprooted from their own people and divorced from their own
culture. Such ministers would be inappropriate for the ministry.
Furthermore, the issue is not just one for Africa or for 'mission
territories'. It is a concern for the church at large. When the
Industrial Revolution brought about major changes in the whole
socio-economic make-up, and hence in general European culture,
there was need of 'indigenisation' for church ministries. The
traditional clergy were no longer in tune with the changes
brought about by industrialisation and urbanisation. Whole
sub-cultures found they were no longer at home in the church
which did not seem to be aware of the changes taking place and
seemed opposed to any social changes. Libermann's insistence
on a local clergy has wider application than might be seen at
first sight. His ideas are explicitly set out in a letter to a French
layman who had a business in Bordeaux. As in the case of clergy
for the colonies, Libermann is much freer to share his new ideas
with a lay person when it comes to changes within the ministry
required for the home front:

> I would like to start a ministry that would embrace all the
> poorer classes. This would be outside the parishes, that is, work
> that the parish clergy would not be engaged in because it is
> outside their ordinary ministry. This ministry would take in
> workers, sailors, soldiers, convicts, prisoners and beggars. For
> this I would like to have houses in the principal ports: Bordeaux,
> Toulon, Marseilles, Brest etc. In these places we would try to
> have a work that would cover everything, not by mixing all
> together, but ministering to each class separately and using
> what is appropriate for each class of people. (ND. IX, 147-148)

We see here a remarkable consistency. If one is really
concerned about a clergy, or rather a ministry, that will be truly

in touch with the people, that understands their problems and speaks their language, then the soldiers, sailors, factory workers, and so many other subcultures needed a relevant ministry. Libermann's idea of ministering to the different groups, not *en masse*, but taking each one separately, would seem to be what was required at that time before the exodus from the church in France began. A century later, when such a movement was tried out in France, then described as *pays de mission*, it was soon suppressed. The Worker Priests movement could have been regarded as an effort to diversify the ministry but it was seen as an attack on the clerical system and was banned.

One of Libermann's early collaborators was a certain M. Luquet. He later joined the French Foreign Mission and was sent to India. He took part in a Synod of Pondicherry in India in early 1844. He was sent to Rome to present the proposals of the Synod. One of the Synod's main concerns was the need for indigenous clergy. It would seem that Luquet was quite influential in Rome and must have had major influence in the Instruction issued by *Propaganda Fide* in 1845, *Neminem Profecto*. This came out clearly on the need for promoting local clergy, insisting that these ought not to be seen as helpers of foreign missionaries but true leaders among their own people. Luquet sent two copies of this to Libermann, and in reply Libermann wrote:

> Now it is to be hoped that all missionaries will work seriously to establish stable churches in the foreign missions. Hopefully, these churches will be put on a par canonically with the churches of Europe and America. For our part, the Instruction strengthens our determination to persevere in our places in Guinea. It will take time to produce results, but it is hoped that we are now working for something stable and permanent. Now we can be assured that we are not just following our own fancies but we are on the lines marked out by the Holy See. (Comp, 68)

This was the kind of leadership Libermann desired from Rome. Mission churches are not to be in any way inferior to those in 'established Christian' lands. The aim of mission is to have them properly and canonically established in a 'stable and permanent' fashion. It is for the central authority in the church to lay down the general framework for the church. Mission has its place within such a framework.

The seminary of the Holy Spirit in Paris had been preparing priests for ministry in the French colonies for over a century. This could have been seen as a truly missionary seminary, in that it was preparing priests for foreign parts. However, Libermann did not share his views. 'This seminary has become, not only useless for the colonies but harmful.' (ND. VII, 84) he wrote.

To help remedy this situation, he established a dialogue with the Archbishop of Paris and the seminary authorities. In this he met with a lot of resistance. The seminary was supported by the government and because of its connection with the colonies had gained government protection when other institutions were banned. French missionaries were part of the whole French colonial set-up. They easily fitted in with the colonial administration.

With the political changes of 1848, however, policy towards the colonies changed, and it became possible for Libermann to take charge of the seminary. In doing this, he became head of the Congregation of the Holy Spirit, founded by Poullart des Places in 1703. His own Congregation of the Holy Heart of Mary ceased to exist canonically.

A seminary that is a kind of training ground for colonial priests was, to Libermann's way of thinking, harmful because it was allied to colonialism which is sinful in its structure. In a long letter to a certain Percin, a black priest from St Lucia who had worked in Haiti, Libermann makes no secret of how he sees this kind of ecclesiastical colonialism:

> The church in Haiti must not be put on the same footing as a church in a mission situation. A civilised country should have a church which is properly organised like all other particular churches that together constitute the universal church. When it has not got this position of respectability among other churches, it is not in a proper position. It is dependent and in disarray. Such dependence and confusion is repugnant to anyone who is concerned with administration. The government must find it distasteful to accept a Prefect Apostolic. (ND. VIII, 335-341)

In Libermann's view, Haiti had every right to independence

from France and from a colonial administration. This held also
for church affairs. An independent government in Haiti could
take umbrage at France deciding who would be in charge of
church affairs, and even in this providing a 'second class'
leadership in the institution of a Prefect Apostolic.

One has to wait for more than a century for the theology of
the local church to get its rightful place. One may wonder if,
after Vatican II, the tendency towards centralisation within the
church is still too strong and some church authorities too fearful
of giving autonomy to the local church. The institution of Papal
Nuncios is often questioned. These are now archbishops and,
especially in third-world countries, seem to have extensive
powers. Governments often complain about foreign embassies
interfering in the affairs of the countries, and with reason.
Likewise, there is reason to suspect that there is frequently too
much interference in church matters by those who are the
ambassadors of the Vatican State. The tendency to over-centralise
is often backed by creating a dependency on foreign aid. Already
in 1849 Libermann, who had no love for Gallicanism, wrote in this
connection:

> The move towards centralisation that has come into church
> administration I regard as unfortunate. This tendency must
> harm the plan of God and the well-being of the church. It
> damages its unity and of its nature tends to divide the
> different parts that according to the institution of Jesus Christ
> should form one compact unity under the Head of the
> church. It is clear that Our Lord did not wish this
> centralisation to be comprehensive. He gave special and
> detailed power to each of the apostles or the bishops, and this
> power was then entrusted to St Peter, the Pope. The
> centralisation willed by Our Saviour is that of the Sovereign
> Pontiff. But this centralisation is not to be concerned with
> every detail. This is simply impossible. Each bishop has
> power as to the details that concern his diocese to the extent
> that this does not conflict with the authority of the Supreme
> Pontiff. Too much centralisation by the bishop in the last
> analysis is schism ... The Spirit of God is not to be found
> where there is too much centralisation. (ND. XI, 97)

His concern for the indigenous clergy is really concern for the establishment of local churches. Haiti should have its own hierarchy; it should be seen as a church that is not in a state of dependence but is truly planted in the soil of Haiti. It simply was unjust for the Archbishop of Paris to claim jurisdiction over the churches of the colonies and oppose any form of decentralisation. Libermann's concern is not so much to formulate a theological position as to propose a way of organising the young churches. His concern, as always, is more with 'orthopraxis' than with 'orthodoxy', though, obviously, both are intimately connected. However, an 'orthodox' position can be challenged when it comes to practical matters of administration and ministry.

If one were to look for the kernel of Libermann's missiology, it would be along the lines of establishing local churches. Mission must aim at building an indigenous church. This applies to situations where new churches are to be established, but also where, because of cultural developments, the church has to move into new areas. When one of his early collaborators complained about the way the congregation was being managed and told Libermann that he was thinking of joining the Jesuits, he was told that 'the Jesuits are without doubt much more capable than we are to form young people, but the Jesuits will never form a local clergy. This is completely at variance with their mission system.' (ND. VII, 232).

Now this could be a very unfair comment regarding Jesuit policy. The point is, however, that this is how Libermann saw the issues and why he continued with his small group of missionaries rather than join up with a much more professional and efficient congregation. He viewed the Jesuits as 'a group that is widely distributed but one that necessarily tends to centralisation'. (ND. VII, 227) And, we have seen, Libermann saw centralisation as being a danger to the church and contrary to the gospel.

After the Revolution of 1848, Libermann saw new possibilities for the colonies. They would no longer be under the French government, at least not to the same extent as before. Though he had, in the past, co-operated with the government in sending priests to the colonies, he now saw a new opportunity, an opportunity for the exercise of more freedom and for establishing a church that would be rooted in the local soil, as he always proposed it should be. He saw now that significant changes were taking place, and he wanted the bishops to be aware of this and not lose a very important opportunity to give the people of the island colonies their own church. After intense negotiations with the Roman authorities, he had got three bishops appointed to the colonies. He hoped these would work for the local churches in the colonies and would have more freedom than the Prefects Apostolic who were subject to the Archbishop of Paris. The policy for these bishops is outlined in a long Memorandum addressed to them in 1849 – The political change in France can be an opportunity for church growth abroad. He wrote:

> Now the day of God's mercy has come for the colonies. Now the clergy is free from subjection to the civil authority, and now black people are free to be Christians, and the white people have lost their power and their wealth and so should be more open to respond to grace and return to God. It is time, now, for the clergy to seriously take on the duties of the priesthood. It is time to be on the move. If the priests are not seriously and zealously concerned with the welfare of the black people it is certain that those who defend the cause of the downtrodden, will see the priests as not being in favour of their plans, and will do all in their power to destroy their influence. (ND. XII, 271)

Here we have a fundamental moral issue. The institution of colonialism is sinful. The domination of one race by another is sinful. The solution is to promote among the subjected people a spirit of freedom where they will find a new vision of life and evolve new structures adapted to their situations. The bishops and priests, if they were to be true to their vocation, had to be on the side of the poor and the oppressed. But taking sides with the poor, for Libermann, meant giving the poor the opportunity to manage their own affairs to the greatest extent possible. A colonial power could often claim to have done much for others, but still left the 'others' in a position of dependence. So a process of education that was truly liberating had to be set up to enable the poor to take their rightful place in their own countries. Earlier, writing to the *Propaganda Fide* and emphasising the need for education, he cites the example of Angola. There, he says, there were local clergy, but 'the education had never really entered into the lives of the people, never developed sufficiently, and so was doomed when the foreign missionaries were no longer there'. (ND. VIII, 234) How the proper system of education could establish, it was not easy to say, and there is a development in Libermann's view all the time. At one time he proposed that:

> The African priests will be educated in Africa, but it might be beneficial for them to do some studies in France so as to rid themselves of some of their former ways and to acquire some European ways that would help them influence their own people when they return home. The black priest will have advantages over the Europeans in many respects with regard to their own people. Left to themselves, they may not persevere for very long nor develop the work as one might hope they would. They will need the guidance and encouragement of the European priests for a time. (ND. VI, 284)

Once it was established that the primary aim of the missionaries was to establish a local church, then whatever was needed to achieve this ought to be attempted. The situation where the missionaries withdrew too soon could lead to the collapse of the work and then, of course, to the cry 'We told you so!' Where the missionary becomes permanently indispensable, this too is not acceptable. A balance has to be struck. Experience is needed in order to be able to strike the proper balance between too hastily retreating and digging in permanently.

The basic principle that Libermann insists on for the establishment of the local church, is that everything possible be done to promote freedom of people. The slaves must be truly liberated, not only in law, but in fact. The African people must be free, not just to do what they like, but to have that sense of worth and dignity so as to be able to see themselves, and be seen by others, as in no way inferior. In a rare philosophical mood, Libermann distinguishes between freedom and independence. People ought to be free. They cannot be independent; they are necessarily interdependent. The churches of Africa and the Caribbean ought to be free but they cannot be independent.

Even the churches of Europe are not independent of their sister churches. As much of what has been discussed so far clearly shows, it is not merely that the 'mission territories' need the help of 'established churches.' For the latter to develop properly, they need to be truly missionary, reaching out to those in need and thereby getting new life from the mission. But as to the freedom, which is absolutely required and the independence that is to be avoided at all costs, we find the following:

> Freedom is given to people by the Creator. Independence is contrary to nature and is destructive of every principle of the Christian faith. The fanatical urge for independence led to Protestantism. It has led, too, to a modem philosophy that promotes egoism to a frightening extent that led to the barbarity of the past century. Christianity has come to bring freedom to the world and at the same time to wage war on independence which is totally contrary to the faith and to moral principles. (ND. X, 231)

This distinction between freedom and independence is rarely considered. It would seem of particular significance. The egoism or individualism of Western culture is often sharply contrasted with the importance of community that one finds in African cultures. The misplaced emphasis on freedom is one that ignores the community dimension of human living. It is true that Christ has made us free. Our freedom is found 'in the one Body of Christ'. We are all members of a body; we cannot be independent of one another, but yet we can be truly free. In a number of different ways, Libermann makes a practical application of this philosophy. Right from the start, he wanted the mission to be the work of a community. If it were left to individuals working independently, it could not succeed. Again, he asked Rome to approve his society. It could not function properly independently of the head of the church, but yet, the society had to have its own freedom to develop and work. The new churches needed their own clergy, but the clergy were not to be trained in an environment that would cut them off from the others; they needed to have lay people with training in different fields to share with them in the building up of the church. Women missionaries were essential for the mission, but Libermann did not consider founding a congregation of nuns but rather worked in close collaboration with a foundress who showed quite an extraordinary sense of freedom of thought and action, Mother Javouhey. The mission could not be independent of the civil authorities either, but it had to collaborate with them and still preserve its freedom. Church and State are mutually inter-dependent. His theorising is rare but Libermann has practical applications for freedom/interdependence dilemma. In a letter to a missionary who wanted government officials to show submission to the church, he writes:

> I ask you to live in peace with the civil authorities and at the same time not do anything unworthy of your priestly ministry and without demeaning yourself. I'm convinced that the government is well disposed towards us. I further believe that it is in our interests to help wherever we can to carry out their wishes. The government views things from a political perspective, of course, but religion has a significant place in this view and can influence policies. Anyhow, even if their views have no relation whatsoever to religion, and that they wish to use religion to achieve their political ends, even this would not justify opposing our views to theirs for both are mutually complementary. (ND. VI, 204-205)

It is understood that the government, *per se*, is not opposed to the church. Furthermore, the autonomy of government in civil affairs is implied. The church finds its role in a society where very many other factors are operating. Again, one has to recognise the freedom of the state in political matters and the freedom of the church in religious matters. In this general atmosphere of freedom, their mutual interdependence is fostered and promoted.

The example of the church in Haiti has been mentioned earlier. This church was something of a test case for Libermann as he tried to set out a practical mission policy. Could the church be in danger of becoming some kind of colonial power? Could there be a danger of the church becoming a foreign power that would hinder the growth of the indigenous people? These were matters that were pondered on in connection with Haiti – the only former colony that had now achieved independence from France:

People have tried to convince me for some time now that the government (of Haiti) is opposed to establishment of the spiritual administration. I believed this myself at one time. But ever since I reflected deeply on this matter, I became convinced that my judgement was premature. It was based on first impressions that unfortunately, are too frequent. According to the present arrangement, Haiti has to accept foreigners for what concerns the spiritual affairs. This arrangement is abnormal. It puts the Haitian church in a chaotic position. The position is wrong, in that nobody from among its own people can become bishop. And then, the personnel needed by the bishop cannot be provided for the diocese and the parishes. The church, then, must depend on foreigners to carry out the ministry.

Is it surprising, then, that the government is creating problems in trying to stabilise the situation? Those who rule the Republic want something that is more in tune with the needs of the country. Haiti needs a bishop and a clergy from among its own. So an interim administration for the diocese is required that will prepare those who would be leaders in the church. (ND. VIII, 335-341)

Even in post-colonial Africa, there are still some who would suggest that this kind of reasoning can have validity in political and economic matters, but where spiritual matters are concerned, such profane reasoning has no place. We are all children of God and all members of one family, it is said – a point that Libermann insisted on. However, there are very legitimate reasons why people should have church leaders from among their people. From what has been discussed in this chapter, it is clear that the ministry to any group of people ought to be attuned to the needs of these people. And a local church needs local leaders. The community of the church is strengthened and encouraged by ministries from among its own members. The dangers to be avoided are subjection and dependence on the one hand and isolation and independence on the other. By trying to identify with the legitimate aspirations of a people, Libermann comes to open up new perspectives in ecclesiology and becomes a pioneer in promoting the idea of free local churches bound together in harmony and love.

Reflection

The beginning of Libermann's mission in the west coast of Africa showed very little promise of success. The American initiative had been abandoned, the missionaries were not prepared for the task and many died within months of arriving and some left for home sick in mind and body. Through all this Libermann was developing a missionary strategy for the church in Africa, utterly convinced that the mission would succeed eventually. The role of the missionaries was to lay the foundation on which African Christians would build. The foundation was basically concerned with a programme of education.

Convinced of the natural goodness of the people, aware of their intelligence being on a par with Europeans, he foresaw local leaders being trained in such a way that they would be competent in promoting the spiritual and material wellbeing of their communities. All programmes, all subjects studied were needed for the building of a stable local church. The material and spiritual were not in opposition but mutually beneficial. Matters of church and state were meant to be distinguished so as to complement each other in promoting the common good of the communities.

The 'integrated' system of education he proposed ought to go a long way in preventing church/state or clergy/laity polarisation. What he proposed with regard to Minor Orders is now taking shape in many places as lay people are involved in church ministries. His ideas on centralisation of authority got plenty of support in Vatican II. Ironically, less centralisation enhances the role of the papacy, just as loss of the Papal States did in the nineteenth century.

CHAPTER SEVEN

The Church in the World

Libermann is not often seen as 'a man of the world'. He led a secluded life. However, when he began a missionary movement his horizons were considerably broadened. When he considered for some time the world of slavery this opened his eyes to a new world – the continent of Africa in particular. In the ghetto of Saverne he had experienced what it was to belong to an ethnic group that was despised and suspect within the larger community. For a time he had taken this for granted as the normal state of things. Then events in France and in his own life brought about a radical change. During the decade of his missionary life he began to move in a different world and tried to adapt to the changed circumstances of life. One aim dominated his life from now on – to help the slaves and the poor of Africa and enable them become citizens of the world.

In trying to procure the maximum help for his mission, he often wrote to government ministries, consulted people in different positions of authority, and took an active interest in world affairs. If one were to compare his correspondence prior to his conversion to mission, to that which can be found in the last few years of his life, one sees an enormous difference. The introvert concerned with personal holiness is now an extrovert who is giving all he has to help the most unfortunate on earth. Personal holiness is now linked in with genuine concern for the welfare of others, the poor and the neglected in particular. The transition from ghetto to the world can be seen in the way others began to consult him and ask his opinion on current affairs.

The last four years of his life are particularly interesting. 1848 was a watershed in French, and even European, politics. Louis Philippe, faced with the fury of a Parisian mob, abdicated. A socialist government came to power. Revolution was in the air all over Europe. Now Libermann was asked by his close confidant,

Gamon, what he thought of the situation. The former adviser is now looking for advice. From his seminary, Gamon now looks to this new missionary for light. This is what he got:

> You asked me what I think of the Revolution. I think that it was an act of God's justice acting against a decadent dynasty that had worked to establish its own power rather than promote the welfare of the people under its care. The pride and pretensions of the regime sought to make it superior to God. It treated the church as a slave. The difficulties of the people were increased, and the people demoralised in order to consolidate its power which moved step by step towards dictatorship. I think that the storm of the French Revolution will overtake them and destroy many of them. The Russian autocrat will have his day too. And another group that was hit by the storm was the aristocratic bourgeoisie that once trampled underfoot the rights of the poor and sold their souls and their country to egoism and self-interest. (ND. X, 144-153)

Where does the self-confidence this passage shows come from? Libermann is not a socialist and he is not an anti-monarchist. He knows that the Revolution brought bloodshed and many deaths. He does not condemn this breakdown of the social system. It was inevitable, it had to happen. It is clear that the source of Libermann's conviction springs from his concern for the poor. The regime had oppressed the poor. It had become power-drunk. It reeked with pride. That such a regime be overthrown is a blessing from God. The wider horizons reached by Libermann's vision centred on the poor and radiated from there. Where the rights of the poor were not respected, then, change had to come or to be brought about.

The church does not necessarily favour a particular form of government. What it ought to strive for is truth and justice. There were many condemnations of Marxism during the second half of the nineteenth century. Not until 1891 did the Pope speak out against injustice in the world and in favour of the rights of the working class. Almost seventy years before the Russian Revolution, we hear that the 'Russian autocrat will have his day'. And if we denounce the terrible horrors perpetrated by the

Russian dictators after 1917, we ought not to ignore the horrors that preceded the communist takeover.

In France elections were to follow the Revolution. And again Libermann is asked if the clergy ought to take part in these elections. So often do we hear that the clergy should keep out of politics, as if non-involvement were not a political option also! It is not any real love for democracy as such that inspires the following reply:

> You ask if the clergy should be involved in the elections. For certain, I believe they owe it to God, to the church and to France to take part. Tomorrow morning I will go to register with all the others who can do so. If all the priests in France took their duties seriously and used their influence to work for the election of leaders in the Republic, then we might have a good Constitution and a good executive of government. And the benefits that could result from this! How many might be saved as a consequence if this choice were made? I realise that the elections are not a church matter, but we must not think that we are still living in the past. The problem with the clergy in recent times is that they have lived in the past. The world has moved ahead. The enemy has aimed his batteries in accordance with the condition and spirit of the times, and we have remained behind. We must keep up with the times while remaining true to the spirit of the gospel. We have to do good and avoid evil as best we can in the conditions and in the spirit of the present time. The forces of the enemy are to be attacked where they are marshalled. They must not be given a chance to consolidate their positions while we look around for them where they no longer are. (ND. X, 151)

We find here the core of Libermann's spirituality. The spirituality of the age when profound changes were taking place called out for the church and its ministers to be awake, watchful and involved. The world is changing and Christians need to be right there trying to bring to this changing world the message of the gospel. To remain static is to fail in one's Christian vocation. The clergy, he says, lived in the past. They are fighting enemies long since dead. New combatants had taken up arms and were given the field. This is the time when modern ideas were being

condemned. In France Lamennais and his group in L'Avenir
were attacking the alliance of throne and altar. Their appeal to
the Pope for support resulted in the encyclical, *Mirari Vos*, of
Gregory XVI which repudiated, among other errors 'that erroneous and absurd doctrine, or delirium, that freedom of conscience
is to be claimed and defended for all men'.

1848 – *The Communist Manifesto*. This was something that did
affect the lives of people and of nations for over a century.
Communism was evil, it was wrong! It should be condemned and
was condemned. What brought it about? Why did it attract
followers? Is there some truth in communism? Is there a warning
and a challenge emanating from the caustic pen of Marx? What is
the response of faith to the growing influence of communism?

> Communism is not to be feared. It will attack and disperse
> riches that have been accumulated. Religion will suffer but a
> temporary setback from the influence of the communist system
> and from the hostility and despotism of some of its leaders. The
> system is not directly in opposition to Christianity. The hatred
> of communists and their programmes are not directly against
> religion, but against capitalism. (ND. X, 182)

The 1848 Revolution in France and throughout Europe, the
rise of communism, the Industrial Revolution were part of life in
the 1840s. These called out to the followers of Christ to be
engaged in the struggle that was taking place in the minds of
people and in the structures of society. To register as a voter is
making a choice. Not to do so is also a matter of choice. The
missionary will move out into the new situation and try and
bring gospel values into areas of life that are new to him. The
battlefield had been abandoned to Marx and his followers for too
long. The church needed a ministry that would be 'indigenous'
to the situation addressed by Marx. But the seminaries had to
maintain the traditional character. The philosophies being taught
were no longer relevant, and theology could be regarded as idle
speculation. This saddened Libermann. He was no longer
impressed by the piety of many of the clergy – a piety that he
once encouraged:

> The vast majority of the clergy are good but in an ordinary
> manner. They are faithful to their duties, they say Mass daily,

faithfully say the office at the prescribed times, they preach,
teach catechism and can be found in the confessional when
they are required to be there. They administer the sacraments
to the sick. The white people are quite happy with this kind
of ministry. They want the priest to be available for them in
the confessional when they come. They want to be left alone
to continue in their indifference and not to be drawn out of it.
(ND. XI, 263-264)

'The white people are happy ...' The rich are happy with the
military junta and pleased when the church does not disrupt the
status quo. But is this a witness to Christ? To ignore the plight of
the poorest in the colonies was seen as sinful. The fact that a
veneer of piety was preserved, that the more influential
inhabitants were very happy with the *status quo*, did not absolve
the clergy from the serious sin of neglecting those who were in
the greatest need. Within the general culture of individualism,
'structural sin' did not seem to have any place, but this is
precisely what is being pointed to here. Such was the ethos of
the clergy that it could be regarded as sinful. This meant that a
new approach was required. And the practical implications of
identifying the sin demanded that something be done.

Among the colonial clergy there were some who gave scandal –
and presumably the white population were scandalised by the
'greed, laziness, impurity' of some priests. But:

The most serious accusation that one could bring against the
colonial clergy is the lack of zeal for the welfare of the black
people. These people are poor, despised, humiliated by their
misfortune and steeped in ignorance and corruption. At the
same time they are wonderfully disposed to return to God
and to hear with respect and love the word of consolation
that the priest ought to bring to them. To abandon such a
people to its misfortune is unpardonable. (ND. XI, 264)

Priests had, in Libermann's view, abandoned their prime
duty of bringing Good News to the poor. This was an unpardonable offence. But it was more than that. It was a sin that cried out
for reparation. If the situation were to be reformed, a certain
number of issues had to be addressed. Three faults had to be

considered in particular. First was the recruitment of the clergy. This was obviously defective. In an earlier chapter we saw how a respected priest, by implication, suggested that 'second class' clergy would be adequate for Africa and how Libermann reacted to this. The idea seemed to be that for work among the poor, for dealing with the uneducated, anything is good enough. The second problem that he suggests as needing attention is the organisation of dioceses. When he dealt with the case of Haiti, he made it clear what he thought should be done in this regard. The third, and by far the most difficult to deal with, was the colonial system itself. The reform of the colonial system would seem to be beyond the competence of the church, but this need not to be the case. To take up a position that would favour the black people, to work for a truly indigenous church, as we have seen, would lay the foundation for the freedom of the colonies. What would not be acceptable was the continuation of a system of clerical respectability, approved by the white people but ignoring the poor.

The Supreme Court of the United States decreed in 1857 that a black person was chattel. In 1847 Libermann realised that:

> The idea of having a coloured priest, and especially a black one, cannot enter the head of any white person in the colonies. Sooner or later this has to change, but there are considerable problems. The clergy will tell you that it is impossible for a white person to confess to a black priest. They even think it would compromise their dignity of the priesthood to admit black priests. I think that it is absolutely impossible to delay the coloured and the blacks from becoming priests. Whatever the difficulties, the problem has to be faced. (ND. XII, 296)

One might wonder how the mindset of the mid-nineteenth century could be found in different ways in the twenty-first century. Are there some people who simply cannot become priests to minister to their own people?

In trying to form priests for his missions, Libermann kept in mind the sinful situations that the priests had to face. Philosophy and theology had to be studied in the seminaries. This was part of the system and was quite acceptable. But there was something more important that required consideration if the priest was to exercise his ministry properly. He realised that knowledge of people and of the social conditions surrounding them was of prime importance:

> One must study carefully the character of the people and examine the tendencies of their hearts, their inclinations and affections. In this way one comes to know their vices and the sources of these vice. (ND. XI, 258)

And to come by this knowledge:

> It is not by a study of philosophy or reasoning that this is acquired but by patient observations under the influence of God's grace. If the missionary is to judge rightly, he must have self-mastery and be inwardly at peace so as to be enlightened by God. Those who strive for this knowledge by their own efforts will often make false judgement in practice. They will be obstinate in judging people and be deluded. Besides, knowledge is not everything. One must adapt to their way of life and the almost infinite variety of characters. This is possible for everyone who keeps his mind and heart open to the light of grace. This knowledge is wholly practical. It consists in a natural tact, perfected by grace that enables one, in a glance, to penetrate into the minds of people. (Gloss 56)

Lest it be thought that Libermann did not favour academic training, it should be noted immediately that he laid down in the Rule that some missionaries, 'a few perhaps, may be able to study the character of the people and articulate this in a scientific manner'. (Ibid) And again, he writes to a missionary, 'We certainly need some missionaries, more talented than others, for ministries that demand more talents and more learning and who could be consulted by their confrères.' (ND. IV, 425) It is readily admitted that missionaries often failed to know the people they were to evangelise and, armed with philosophy and theology, imposed systems that had little or nothing to do with the gospel and were totally at variance with the culture of the people. It is true also that many missionaries did have a wonderful rapport with their people, developed an appreciation for their culture and their way of life and were able to relate naturally, one might say, with people, and in this way the growth of the local churches made progress. This way of knowing people was what Libermann called 'practical' and was the knowledge that was required of all missionaries. Knowing people, appreciating their culture, sharing their way of life is not the preserve of professional anthropologists.

As in our own time, there were then some philanthropists anxious to help the people of Africa. One such organised group was *La Compagnie d'Afrique*. It started in 1845. A year later Libermann wrote to the secretary:

> The mission does not consist solely in the message of faith that we proclaim but also in the initiation of the people to our European civilisation. Faith, Christian morality, education, knowledge of agriculture and trades, all complement one another and promote and strengthen each other. In this way, little by little they bring the black people to share in the benefits of Christianity and the civilisation of the people of Europe. (ND. VIII, 318)

More will be said later about the 'civilisation' that is mentioned here. For the present, it is clear that Libermann was concerned with a general education system embracing literacy, agriculture, technical skills, etc. Then he hoped that he could co-operate with others who professed to help the Africans. In this case it did not work; he said the advice he got from the secretary was of very little worth, and there seemed to be no further contact. However, the fact that help and co-operation was sought indicated what kind of mission was being planned. The Good News to the poor was not merely something that has become very common, something that is supported by a number of transnational companies today, and that could rightly be regarded as the opium of the masses. 'Being saved', 'born again' can have a profound effect on people, it is true, but if the proclamation of salvation does not take the social, political and economic realities into account, then it could be a travesty of the gospel. The missionary imperative is always to consider the good of the people in their particular circumstances. To get people 'saved' and not to consider literacy and general education would be to ignore an element of Good News that the people of African ought to share.

Many aspects of European 'civilisation' would benefit Africa, but by no means all. In a long letter to a community in Africa, Libermann tries to spell out what the community had to aim at:

> Do not give too much credence to what is said by those who travel along the coast when they tell you about the people they have met, even if they have lived there for many years. Listen to what they say, but don't let that distort your judgement. These people look at issues from their own point of view and with their own prejudices. I'm sure you will judge the people in a different manner from those who speak about them. You know that if we had paid attention to what was the consensus of those who should have given us information regarding the black people of the colonies, information that was thought to be very sound, we would never have begun our mission to Bourbon and Mauritius. However, our men have done marvels there. They have learned and judged quite differently from those others who spoke to us. Do not judge by first impressions. Do not act according to what you have seen in Europe nor according to European customs. Get rid of Europe, its customs and its spirit. Become black with the blacks, and then you will know them as they should be known and not the way they are known by Europeans. Let them be themselves. Become their servants. As servant, adapt to their customs and their way of life. Do all this with the aim of improving them, sanctifying them, ennobling them, and gradually forming them into God's people. That is what St Paul means by becoming all things to all in order to win all for Christ Jesus. (ND. IX, 330)

How can one make an 'objective' assessment of humans? One could say that objectivity in knowledge of people is simply not possible. People are not, must not be thought of, as 'objects'. Hence, to know a person is to establish a relationship with such a person. One can learn, of course, from others about certain ways of behaving, customs, language etc. But there is something over and above this required of the missionary. In the final analysis, the missionary is concerned with helping, but those being helped are never the 'objects' of his care. This missionary outlook might well be considered by many today. The international agencies, World Bank, IMF, United Nations Agencies and transnational companies, as well as 'developed' countries, have their experts who have studied the situations and with considerable learning have devised solutions to the many problems of Africa, and yet, one might wonder if they really know what they are about. Too often the subjects of development, the people themselves, are not known, and hence, so many laudable purposes are frustrated. One might say that some know a great deal *about* people, but do not know the people.

The church has a duty to society. It is part of society and ought to give a particular orientation to all aspects of life. Libermann was interested above all in the development of people, development of the 'character' of people. This would form the basis of all development. When missionaries had set up a training institute in Africa and the work there seemed to be prospering, the missionaries are reminded of their primary duty. To develop the 'character' of the people:

> Help them to appreciate the beauty of freedom and the equality they share with all the children of God. All ideas of inferiority must be got out of their minds. This would weaken them and debase them in their own eyes. Study their character, their mentality, their fundamental vision of life. (ND. IX, 360)

What must worry educationalists at present is the tremendous advance in so many fields of life and at the same time, the thought that the 'character' of people may not be improved with all the advances in education. One cannot help noticing among the people of so-called 'developed' countries the lack of balance between academic achievements and personal growth. And again, with some experience, one can find in Africa great strength of character (that indefinable quality in the present context) where there has been little or no formal education. There are forms of education that destroy character, that damage people.

Freedom is certainly emphasised today. How new is this emphasis? The missionary is exhorted to promote the freedom of the young people in school. And the key to true freedom is in the 'character' of the person. It is not so much in the rules, regulations or the lack of same. Freedom is in the person. It can be so easy for the missionary to have 'subjects' but not so easy to have brothers and sisters of Jesus and be one of the children of God in the family. Was the church to the fore in the quest for freedom from colonialism?

The missionary is an odd type. He must be careful not to adhere too easily to any form of conventional wisdom. Airports, roads, factories and offices certainly have a place in society. But there is something else, more important, but may not be easily detected outside the general concept of development. Africa has now got many experts in different disciplines who are in no way inferior to their counterparts around the world. One ought to be glad and rejoice that such is the case. What might be questioned is how rarely the experts enhance the dignity of others. Libermann's concern that the teacher could make the unschooled feel inferior needs to be taken to heart today. The preacher in the pulpit, the District Officer at a public meeting, the party hopeful on the campaign, the chairman of a small Christian Community, are all too liberal with their advice on what should be done and what should be avoided.

The missionary has to be wary of the generous donor. As a critic of the handouts, of international loans, of imported experts, he puts himself out on a limb. When many may be advocating increase in foreign aid, the missionary has to be circumspect and suggest that perhaps an increase in the price of coffee, tea, sisal, fruit etc, might be of greater benefit. But this would not be a popular line to take. The scene has changed over the past century, and perhaps there is no need to elaborate any further on what should be done. Africans now speak for Africa. They are now responsible for the spiritual and material welfare of their people. The missionaries and colonial administration brought a large variety of systems to Africa. Inevitably some do not fit. An inordinate sense of pride and superiority was something that did not befit a missionary. Libermann found an example of this.

A case arose where a government officer was invited to attend the opening of a new church building. He turned up with quite an entourage of soldiers. The zealous missionary became furious at the sight of Muslims and 'infidels' present at such a sacred function and let his mind be known to the officer in question, who took offence. But the missionary was delighted with his stand for God and let his superior in Paris know how he had witnessed to the true faith. He may have been more than surprised to receive the following reply:

> Yes, the African mission requires that we have dealings with officials. It would be very unfortunate if these officials got the impression that you were opposed to the government. Don't get mixed up in politics. Don't bear any grudge in your heart against these fellows. Let them know that if you have a different view, this is a matter of conscience for you. Do not speak and act with authority, I mean by putting on an air of authority. On no account are you to humiliate others. It is normal for soldiers to act on impulse. It is quite natural for soldiers to assert their authority by the use of force, with violence and pride. They have not worked at acquiring evangelical perfection. (ND. IX, 239)

The military mind, the ethos of the army, the ethics of business, the morals of medicine, the world of politics, all these often remain outside the normal reflections of the priest. And yet there is a Christian imperative to go out to these 'foreign' lands and make disciples in these 'nations' also. One does not have to be a doctor to know what it is to be sick. One need not be a soldier to have some idea of how a soldier is trained to behave. From his relatively secluded environment, Libermann could see that to 'put on an air of authority' when faced with the military was neither sensible nor evangelical. It was not at all effective. This was just a practical case where the practical realities of life required the priest to try and reach out to a 'foreign' and seemingly hostile environment and find a way of dealing with it. The mission to the slaves and to Africa opened up other 'missions' and especially opened up minds to areas that needed to be evangelised. The early Christians debated whether a Christian could join the army. Today one wonders whether it is possible for a true Christian to enter the world of politics, business, arms manufacture, stock exchange etc. It would seem that shunning these in order to 'save one's soul' could be an option for some, but for the church in general, it is imperative to be involved in whatever pertains to human life. Sending missionaries to Africa seemed to some to be sending them to an early grave and on a mission doomed from the outset. Africa was God's creation; the people were God's children; not to accept the call would have been a betrayal of Christ and his church. The world of politics might seem to be dangerous, and the business person might wonder if the gospel is applicable in the market place of today, but there lies the challenge. The world needs the gospel, and the gospel needs to enlighten the world. Risks there are aplenty, but the Founder of Christianity risked his life and seemed to fail.

Reflection

Throughout his 'missionary' period Libermann judged the regimes from the perspective of the poor. He was always ready to deal with the civil authorities and showed no overt hostility towards them. Generally he kept his political opinions to himself. Only to the close confidant, Gamon, do we find him expressing himself so passionately. He was aware of the growing interest in communism and its concern for the oppressed. It was something the church ought to consider. Likewise, he sensed the demise of the monarchy and saw opportunities for the church to support democracy. The traditional alliance of throne and altar had changed. Many from among the clergy yearned for a return to the *ancien régime*.

Young people now seem to be drawn to work for justice. Interest in evangelisation seems to be low. Have we a false dichotomy here? Is the notion of evangelisation too restricted in the minds of people? Spirituality appears to be associated with devotional practices and tends to be introspective. Newspapers, radio and TV were not allowed for seminarians in the past.

CHAPTER EIGHT

Christianity and 'Civilisation'

David Livingstone's mission was to bring Christianity, commerce and civilisation to Africa. One cannot read the letters of Libermann concerning his mission without coming up against the question of 'civilisation'. It has to be admitted that the term 'civilisation' has the taint of political incorrectness nowadays but the word is so frequently used that Libermann's notion of the term must be explored. About this we continue to let him speak for himself, hoping that the many different nuances of meaning, depending on the one being addressed, will become clear. He was a man of his time. In some ways he was ahead of his time. For him 'civilisation' may not have the same connotations as it has today. One thing will become clear. The gospel message was not seen as something that could be imparted in its 'pure' state, as it were. The missionary, in order to be true to the gospel, had to be concerned with the 'civilisation' that was part and parcel of the gospel. Writing to Louverture, Libermann set out his ideas for the 'evangelisation and civilisation' of Africa. Already we have seen that the institutions that Libermann wished to set up in Africa would be concerned with education on a wide variety of subjects: religion, morality, agriculture, mechanics, trade etc. Such schools would be instruments of bringing 'civilisation' to Africa.

> Religion will influence their minds and their morals. It will develop in them a spiritual and supernatural well-being. Civilisation will influence their social and civil life and help them to achieve natural well-being. (ND. VI, 66)

The two-tier, natural/supernatural is part of the thinking of the time. Yet in this context we can see that they are not separable elements in the lives of people. The same schools aim at helping people grow as people, and for this the whole person has to develop. The dichotomy, natural/supernatural, is overcome in a very practical way. Education includes development of the potentialities of the person. But what kind of civilisation is to be imported into Africa? Libermann was conscious of Africans having some form of spirituality. In his view this would be very deficient and would need to be developed. He was conscious also about a kind of 'civilisation' or culture that permeated European thought and action and he had his misgivings about this too.

> It is of the greatest importance that the civilisation brought to these countries produce a deep unity among the indigenous people. If it brings disorder, they are not being offered any gift of value. For this unity to be brought about there has to be a unifying foundation which is to be had only in religion. To bring to Africa irreligion, immorality and the many vices so sadly found among the working classes with civilisation, then it would be far better to leave them in their uncivilised state. (ND. VI, 66)

It is worth nothing that 'civilisation' through the schools ought to aim at bringing unity to the people. Perhaps Libermann is aware of the terrible divisions that brought about the Revolution in France. The divisions that resulted from these were still very much alive in France and would lead to another revolution within a few years. Education should not be for the formation of elite. Elitism is divisive. Education, as we have seen, is not for the formation of a clergy who would be cut off from their people. The liberty, fraternity and equality that the Revolution stood for ought to be promoted from the beginning. The very basis of unity is religion. Religion, then, ought to permeate the whole system, providing that all-important sense of unity among the people. Libermann knew the black people were despised by many Europeans. Likewise, he thought that they were equally despised in their own eyes. It would be disastrous, then, if in trying to give them a sense of their dignity, some were educated in such a way as to look down on their own people.

In his Memorandum to *Propaganda* in 1846, he has a whole section entitled: 'Basis for a civilisation not depending on the presence of missionaries.' Already the title suggests that whatever 'civilisation' might be brought by missionaries, what should emerge eventually is a culture that is truly indigenous and that does not depend on foreigners for support. In order to impress on *Propaganda* the importance of this particular civilisation, he refers to the situation of Angola and the Congo in the sixteenth century:

> Religion once prospered there. There were then the beginnings of a civilisation. But now the country has reverted to barbarism. We believe, however, that this relapse is not due to something inherent in the people, but rather to the policy being followed in the establishment of the mission. The new bishop should not have been content with a flying squadron of missionaries. He should have formed an indigenous clergy and a hierarchical organisation indigenous to the country. Because he did not attempt this, the disintegration of Christianity is not hard to understand. (ND. VIII, 234)

The civilisation that brings stability, then, cannot be that which needs external support. It may be imported, but must be appropriated by the people; it must not remain a foreign entity. To have a system that will place people in a permanent state of dependence is something that must be avoided. If the seed brought by the missionary is not adapted to the native soil, then there can be no hope of a harvest. He continues to insist on this to *Propaganda* when considering the failure of the Congo mission.

> The civilisation was really weak. At its best, it never really penetrated into the people. Furthermore, a civilisation that is not accompanied by reasonably well-developed education is but an illusion. It is the implanting of a civilisation that is doomed to failure. It will disappear with the decline of faith and the absence of foreign priests. This civilisation was but a mediocre knowledge of agriculture and of trades and of small business. It imparted a degree of knowledge that did not take root among the people and, therefore, could only be of minimal assistance to them. The civilisation had to fail, because it did not penetrate into the people; it was not brought to a level of perfection by study and the practice of religion. (ND. VIII, 236)

Civilisation, then, is not a veneer. It must be something that 'penetrates into the people.' (The expression is rather crude, but it emphasises an important reality: it has to be integrated into the whole culture of the people and become part of their way of life.) To speak a foreign language, wear foreign clothes, adopt foreign manners etc, would be putting on a veneer, whereas something deeper is required, something different has to be achieved. The people must feel at home with civilisation and must not be simply aping something that is foreign to them.

The civilisation in question is brought about by education. The system of education that is envisaged must not be superficial. It must aim at the integral development of the people. The only experience Libermann can call upon indicates that a superficial teaching of Christianity is not enough. There is need to have a more thorough system and one adapted to the cultural climate of the people. The implication in the Memorandum is that *Propaganda* should have a policy in this regard to give direction to the missionaries. There is no reference to the experience of the Jesuit missionaries in India and China!

Frequently projects are initiated to promote the 'development' of Africa that in time collapse and leave an atmosphere of disillusionment. How often too are the Africans blamed for neglecting 'development' when in fact, what is being presented cannot truly 'penetrate into their lives', cannot really form part of, and be integrated into their way of life. Democracy, for instance, is something that is required for Africa by most foreign powers. But can it really be integrated into their way of thinking and living? Is there not an intolerable arrogance being displayed by many today who insist on forms of government that may have no foundation in the culture of the people? Again, institutions and structures have been put in place, and often it is found that they need foreigners to keep them functioning. Significantly, Libermann insisted that any civilisation brought to Africa must not depend on foreigners for its continuity and prosperity.

One might wonder about the need for inculturation in the Catholic Church of Africa today. How much depends on directives from outside in matters of liturgy, church structure, forms of prayer etc? Inevitably, missionaries brought what they considered essential. But after a time, it may seem that what was imported was not appropriate to the way of life of the African people. There is the further question about the diversity of Christian denominations and churches. Why such fragment-ation among Christians? Where is the unity that Libermann regarded as of the greatest importance?

The question of relationship between Christianity and colon-ialism often arises. For Libermann, the danger of ecclesiastical colonialism had to be avoided. This is why he stressed the need for a system of evangelisation that would not require the indefinite presence of missionaries. The missionary had to have a policy from the beginning to establish the church in such a way as to be adapted to the culture and be able to survive when he leaves. The stability required would be ensured by working for a civilisation that was based on 'religion, education and work'. (ND. VIII, 248)

The civilisation in question had to aim at providing self-sufficiency. The people must be expected from the start to aim at being able to manage their own affairs. Hence, 'it is not enough to show them how the work is to be done, they must be taught the theory so that they will be in a position to do without the help of the missionaries'. (ND. VIII, 248) If the people are not given the 'theory,' that is, if the system of education is not adequate, then they will remain in their 'infancy and revert to their primitive condition when the missionaries leave'. To establish the faith, and the culture that integrates the faith into the way of life of the people, 'will take some time. But it will never be achieved unless from the very beginning it is aimed at. At first, the efforts will necessarily be imperfect.' (Ibid) One must aim at helping people to be self-sufficient from the start. The process will take time, but the aim must be adhered to. There must be no compromise in the policy of setting up an indigenous ministry and self-sufficient society.

The 'Incarnational' approach to evangelisation is stressed in the Memorandum. The plan being proposed, he claims, is underpinned by two mutually dependent principles:

The first: we consider that faith cannot have a stable form among these people nor can the young churches have any security for their future without the support of a civilisation that has been developed to a considerable extent. Furthermore, it seems to us that the development and consolidation of the churches of Europe was brought about by a developed civilisation. The second principle is that civilisation is impossible without faith. (ND. VIII, 248)

The dichotomy between the natural and the supernatural, between the material and the spiritual is overcome in the very practical implementation of an integral programme of evangelisation. However theologians might expound these relationships, it was vital that the missionaries did not apply a 'two-tier' system. 'It is the duty of the missionary, it is his bounden duty, to work not only in the domain of morals but also in the intellectual and physical fields, that is, in education, in agriculture and trades'. (Ibid) Cultural changes are inevitable in the process of integral evangelisation. The educational system and the religious beliefs and practices must necessarily bring about considerable change. There is no opposition to change, as such. 'The civilisation that consists of a mediocre knowledge of agriculture and trades and small business could not really take root among the people nor be of any great advantage to them.' (Ibid) The civilisation of dependence and inferiority could not be part of a truly Christian civilisation:

Those who have a low opinion of themselves and who have no grasp of their dignity nor of the destiny to which they are called cannot have the determination to advance. Their minds must be enlightened, their hearts and wills strengthened by what the faith teaches regarding their origin and destiny. (Gloss 56)

The theological truths concerning the equality of all people, the creation and eternal destiny of all people had to be taught, not just by repeating the formulae, but especially by the civilisation that was being introduced. If an inferior system of education were introduced, then the basic equality of peoples would be contradicted, and the message given would be that the Africans were inferior. The civilisation in question is not something static. It aims at change, change for the better. A vital element in the process is the change in self-image. The people must see and feel their dignity in the depths of their being.

In writing to a community in Dakar in 1847, Libermann spells out in concrete terms what he means by civilisation. He is aware of what this means to Europeans. He is aware of what is being said about Africa and Africans. The Christian's vision ought to be different:

> Do not judge according to what you have seen in Europe nor according to what you have been accustomed to in Europe. Get Europe out of your system; get rid of its customs and its mentality. Become black with the blacks, and you will judge them as they ought to be judged and not according to European standards. Allow them to be themselves. (ND. IX, 326)

This must be considered one of the finest pieces of advice to missionaries. And it has universal application. It is crystal clear that the civilisation Libermann speaks of is not something that has to be imported from Europe. In the general view of mission that has been portrayed here, the instructions here are entirely valid. Evangelisation today does not mean imposing a culture from the past and traditions that no longer have validity. A liturgy and spirituality that was appropriate in the last century may not be what is required today. Statements of doctrine that were perfectly orthodox and acceptable in the thirteenth century may need to be adapted to the people of a technological society of the twentieth century.

When one missionary took pride in having resisted French military officers, Libermann was not too pleased. He thought that one has to enter into their ways of thinking and dealing with them on their own terms. The military culture had to be taken into account:

> Haven't you been too severe, too tenacious? Have you not lacked the appropriate way of dealing with them. Adapt to the habits and customs of all, and do not expect others to adapt to your tastes and customs ... Those who are charged with the salvation of people should know how to adapt to others without, however, being broken or breaking others. (ND. VII, 161)

'Not broken and not breaking others' is significant. The

missionary who suffers from culture-shock is not what is required. He needs to have a degree of maturity and self-confidence if he can relate to others of a different culture. But the inflexibility that will insist on having others conform is contrary to the true missionary spirit. So a missionary is told how to behave with government. 'If you have to disagree let it be known that it is a matter of conscience, but avoid speaking with authority, I mean affected authority, and on no account humiliate others'. (ND. IX, 239)

One could see the application of the doctrine of the Incarnation outlined here. Jesus became one of us, took on our human nature so as to divinise it. Let the Africans be African. Get Europe out of your system, and do what you can to serve the people. This is not easy. He had pointed out that the example of Europeans could lead to taking a posture of superiority towards them, and human respect could prevent some missionaries from treating them with love and affection. The self-emptying of Jesus is the model for the missionary. The haughty disdain of the settler cannot reveal the face of Jesus to others.

When a school had been set up and boys had been enrolled, Libermann wrote to the priest in charge of the school. The letter gives an idea of what he meant by the civilisation which the missionaries were expected to bring to Africa:

I hope the boys will profit from the training they are now getting. Try to develop their character, promote what is good in them and use this to educate them properly. Perfect what is good, correct what is defective, and develop whatever energy they have. Take care when I say you should correct them. I do not mean you should scold them all the time. Rather, try prudently to use every means to free them from their faults without making them develop other defects. By correcting faults in a faulty manner, other faults often result. Inspire them with self-respect. Help them to understand that they are free; help them appreciate this freedom – the beauty of the freedom and equality which they share with all the children of God. Try to remove from their minds any idea of inferiority. This would exacerbate their natural weakness and give them a low self-image.

Once they come to realise that they are in no way inferior by nature to Europeans, when they become convinced in a practical experiential way, in the depths of their souls, they will be all the more inspired to work for the salvation and the advancement of their own people. If they come to be convinced that their own race can and will become equal to Europeans as regards development of the mind, they will be inspired to rescue their people from the sad condition they are in.

Make a study and penetrate deeply into the character, the mentality and the basic attitudes of the black people. Avoid judging them by outward appearances. This leads to superficial judgements that led many astray. But on the other hand, avoid premature enthusiasm. Don't make hasty judgements; do not see everything as bright and fair. There is no doubt the Africans have their faults, just as the Europeans have theirs. They have their strong points too, like the Europeans have. (ND. IX, 359-361)

The Africans must not be expected to be simply like the Europeans. They have their own 'character' which needs to be carefully studied but, above all, developed according to its own particular nature. Libermann was aware that changes in the lives of African people would take place as a result of the political, commercial and religious influences coming to the continent. He welcomed some changes and wanted to be part of the transforming process. The missionary would find his place among a number of different agencies that would bring about significant transformation in African society. The missionary had to be part of the transforming process. He had to be conscious of his distinctive role and to be aware of the dangers of being diverted from this. Not everything being brought to Africa would be to the advantage of the African people.

Several societies, commercial and humanitarian, are actively involved and the most powerful European powers are bringing considerable resources to bear on the civilisation of these people ... We consider that these movements, in working for the good of the people could well be disastrous for their souls. (ND. VIII, 224)

So the missionary priest has to be clear on his role.

> Every priest is ordained simply for the salvation of people. It
> happens at times, however, that in the colonies the priests
> can allow themselves to be influenced by human points of
> view in his dealing with the black people. They want to form
> people before forming Christians. This is a gross error.
> People are not formed except by Christianity, its laws and its
> practice. (ND. XII, 273)

'Civic education' in Libermann's estimation, need not be the
concern of the priest. Religious education, properly understood,
must include civic and other branches of education. Religious
education is not to be seen as divorced from the political, social
and commercial concerns of people. Religion, properly
established, ought to impact on every aspect of life. Nothing
human is foreign to the gospel. Religion should be an integral
part of the total culture of people.

Religion should transcend national differences. When it was
proving very difficult to get French missionaries into Mauritius,
a British territory since 1815, Libermann sought the aid of
Cardinal Wiseman in trying to persuade the British government
to change policy. For his part, Libermann was willing to have
these French priests take on British citizenship. 'We are prepared
to give up everything for the salvation of the people in the
missions. We avoid all political involvement in order to promote
the glory of God and the salvation of souls'. (ND. X, 199) How
much was a missionary expected to give up? This was not easy to
determine in practice. One of the early missionaries was told to
'adapt to the customs and way of life of the people and don't try
to make them conform to your tastes and customs. (ND. VII, 161)

To some extent this same principle had to apply to dealing
with governments. Flexibility had to be practised when the
welfare of the people was at stake and no basic principle was
being compromised. It was time for the missionary to make
amends for some of the injustices of the past. The black people,
Libermann admitted 'have suffered so much from us, proud
Europeans that it would be a source of great happiness for me to
make amends for some of the injustices the whites have inflicted

on them'. (ND. IX, 158) The imposition of a 'white' culture, even if this were possible would add another injustice to the long list.

'Inculturation' was not in Libermann's vocabulary. He did not work out a theory of how the message of the gospel could best be integrated into the African culture. This would be the work of missionaries who would relate to the African people in a truly Christian way. He was able to appreciate how the true notion of inculturation works, however. Mother Javouhey had sent three young men from Senegal to be trained in the colonial seminary in France. Libermann was impressed with one of them in particular.

> This young man has an excellent personality, energetic and not lacking in intelligence. Although he has spent many years in Europe, he has not been too Europeanised. So there is every hope that he will easily adjust to this own people when he returns home. He is infinitely less imbued by European ideas than is M. Seclau. (ND. IX, 335)

The idea that being 'civilised' meant becoming more like Europeans was far from Libermann's idea of civilisation. He had the wisdom to recognise that an African could be educated, could spend many years away from his own people and still be authentically African. He realised that there was something amiss when one lost touch with one's culture and adopted the veneer of a foreign culture. However, he wished that Africans could be educated, could be creative, and could develop their God-given talents in such a way as to be an inspiration for their own people.

A certain ambiguity can be detected in some African writers who are full of praise for African culture and deplore the havoc done by missionaries to this culture. Such a stance is understandable and healthy up to a point. It can happen that some of these scholars do not fully appreciate the desire of many traditional Africans to share in the opportunities for study that these have had. The beauty of African culture can be viewed differently by the academic and the man or woman in the village who has never been to school. Moreover, the scholar who is more at home in a foreign country or who writes for a foreign readership may need to protest too much because of a certain loss of cultural identity.

Libermann had the experience of trying to integrate into the life of post-Revolutionary France from the Jewish ghetto. He was a Frenchman who did not know French! He would remain a Jew, but with a difference. He realised that there were cultural problems in Europe and would have wished to provide clergy to deal separately with different sub-cultures – 'workers, sailors, soldiers, prisoners and even beggars in the main coastal towns (of France)'. (ND. IX, 147) For him, civilisation was concerned with helping people develop their potential in the light of the Resurrection of Jesus and the living presence of the Holy Spirit. This could best be carried out in a community environment. He suggests that a missionary try 'to form an association of workers ... and not to forget the women. An association of women could be established ... who could eventually advise on the education of girls' but these suggestions are put forward 'with a certain timidity not knowing enough about the conditions of the country'. (ND. X, 140)

Culture is dynamic. 'Civilisation' is constantly changing. The challenge for the missionary was first of all to know the people, to empathise with them and to bring the message of the gospel to them. The gospel would demand change. The missionary would have to be in one way or another, an agent for change. The worlds of business, of communications, of technology, of entertainment have brought about enormous cultural changes, not only in Africa but throughout the world. New forms of slavery have to be confronted today by a civilisation of love and justice. The gospel has to meet the challenges of the trans-national corporations, of the drug barons, of the media magnets and of the culture of death that is part of modern life. The mission to bring Good News to the slaves of today presents a challenge. Libermann may have something to contribute to this mission. We try to explore the potential that this could have.

Reflection
Libermann was aware to some extent of the differences between the way of life of Africans and Europeans. His own experience would have taught him the cost of change from the Jewish ghetto to becoming a 'liberated' Frenchman. To be cut off from his own people and especially cursed by his father might have

been the cause of his epilepsy. At the time of revolutions in France cultural changes were common.

Missionaries would find they had to cross cultural barriers in their ministry. To implement the school system would bring about change. The preaching of the gospel begins with a call to repentance; to a change of heart and mind. The gospel message is always 'packaged' in some cultural wrapping. It can be difficult to distinguish between the message and the cultural context but the missionary must try to distinguish.

Culture is empirical. It is not normative. A closed society tends to see its way of life as normative, as the right way. A dominant culture can assume that it is the right one and the one that should be adopted by all. For the Victorians to be civilised was to be British! For many to be Catholic is to be Roman. The missionary is often in a dilemma, trapped between cultures. Jesus lived as a faithful Jew but his life and his teaching can ennoble and challenge all cultures.

CHAPTER NINE

Mission then and now

In the preceding chapters I have given a brief summary of the mission of Libermann from his conversion to mission in 1839 up to his death in 1852. During that period his concern was with the African people, initially those who were enslaved and later those in the continent of Africa. Libermann's world is vastly different from ours and still his missionary journey has a message for us today. It was with this in mind that the study was done in the first instance, with the young churches of Kenya in mind. Some experience in Africa helped to confirm the value of what can be called a 'missionary' apostolate. Now it is possible that the message from a different time and place can have some relevance for Ireland. Obviously a good deal of critical assessment has to be applied to allow for the different time and culture.

There is a growing realisation that a missionary task faces the Catholic Church in Ireland. The insight of Vatican II that 'the church by its very nature is missionary'[1] needs to be applied now in a practical way. In the past the missionary apostolate was performed 'in pagan lands afar'. In this sense the Irish have been truly missionary. A missionary outreach continues in different ways by various organisations. NGOs have taken up where religious congregations were once to the fore. The challenge now is from the home front. Here something more needs to be done to move from church maintenance to mission outreach.

Libermann's mission at first was concerned with people in the margins of the society. Many slaves were baptised but not evangelised. He saw the slaves as belonging to a Catholic country – France. He became aware of another marginalised category –

---

1. *Ad Gentes*, 2

the factory workers in the cities. For them a mission was needed also 'to include the poorer classes'. (p 78) His missionary vision was inclusive of *ad extra* and *ad intra*. He saw France as 'mission territory' a century before the question was seriously raised by Abbé Godin in the 1940s. The mission territory is found at home and abroad. A few issues are taken to explore a way of dealing with the home mission.

Communication

The sources from which Libermann's missionary thinking is taken are his letters and memoranda. What might be called his systematic writing has scarcely been used. One of these is *Instructions aux Missionaires*[2] which attempts to give a detailed orientation to his missionaries. He began the writing of the *Instructions* on Monday of Holy Week, 14 April 1851. He had less than ten months to live. He had planned 38 chapters but only 5 were completed. By the beginning of December his health was so poor that he could not continue the work. It would seem that the project was too much for him, given his state of health, his limited theological training, and not having practical experience of the conditions of the missionaries in Africa. After making a number of attempts to draw from this, the efforts were abandoned. The material is there but it is so wrapped in convoluted 'theology' that communication breaks down. Where one finds Libermann in clear decisive fashion is in his letters, and memoranda to a lesser extent.

His letters to individuals and memoranda show very keen insights into the characters of his correspondents; his advice is balanced, with commonsense and mature judgement. When writing a treatise he gets out of his depth and the result is usually disappointing. His theology is limited to a seminary course of that time and is uninspiring as it is faulty. The spirituality taught in the seminary was that of the French School. This may have influenced him at one time but he changed considerably when his missionary project was under way and he was dealing with real-life situations.

The economist and writer, Kenneth Galbraith, frequently refers to what is trite and irrelevant as 'theological'. How much of modern writing on religious subjects is 'theological'? How much is relevant outside the circle of writers? Has a gap opened between theologians and pastoral workers? Is it left to the media and their Religious Affairs Correspondents to fill the gaps?

Significant progress has been made in 'scientific' theology especially in scripture and in communicating new developments in religious thinking. Theology has moved from the seminaries to secular third-level institutions. This is a positive sign and broadly in line with Libermann's idea of a school where religion would be one subject in the syllabus. In this scheme it would have to dialogue with other disciplines. Very significant developments in Libermann's thinking occurred when he moved out of a ghetto. Perhaps theologians need to examine where they are with regard to their communication with contemporary cultures.

Conversion

The missionary apostolate of Libermann began with a conversion. It might not have been as dramatic as what he experienced at baptism; he speaks of 'a little spark'. Whatever its intensity it brought about an important change in his life. He saw slaves in a new light that spurred him to act. They were no longer slaves for him but children of God, brothers and sisters of Jesus Christ. The wretched of the earth ought to know this and be enabled to appreciate it in their lives.

Libermann had always been a 'spiritual' person. His conversions were not from being 'bad' to becoming 'good'. Denis McBride, a scripture scholar and a gifted communicator, says that conversion is from seeing things in a new way. For example: Husband: 'I'm going to the bank'. Wife: 'No, you're not. It's a bank holiday.' New knowledge or insight brings about some change. 'I have left Rennes ...'

His conversion to mission brings a significant change to his spirituality. This has been noticed by some scholars. Fr J. Lecuyer C.S.Sp. wrote:

> It may be useful perhaps to conclude by seeking to place him among other schools of spirituality. L. Cognet and P. Blanchard have pointed out Libermann's links with the so-called

French School. True, in the beginning he often quoted M. Olier and recommended people to read him, while at Rennes he studied St John Eudes. Later, however, references to these two disappear almost completely. The gospels and St Paul become more and more the sourcebooks from which he draws and which he quotes constantly.[3]

Michael Cahill has made a convincing case to show the very little influence Libermann's Rabbinical studies had on his Commentary on John's gospel.[4] When he embraced Christianity Libermann appears to have abandoned the past in as far as that was psychologically possible. I suspect that a somewhat similar experience occurred when his conversion to mission happened. When he left Rennes he left aside the seminary spirituality of the French School. In this connection P. Sigrist, echoing Lecuyer, writes:

After leaving Issy and Rennes, we are surprised to find that references to Olier and John Eudes disappear almost entirely in Libermann's writing. It is the same with any significant correspondence with his former mentors. We see him spiritually transformed; he becomes more flexible, less pessimistic and freer.[5]

He goes on to say that the absence of references to many popular devotions is striking.

The changes mentioned here could have relevance today. The Jewish ghetto and Sulpician seminaries were closed societies. To move outside their confines was to see a different world. Ireland was quite insular and tightly controlled. De Valera in politics, John C. McQuaid in church affairs, symbolised the closed society in Ireland during the post-war years. The revolt against authority, started by students and taken up in society

---

3. Quoted from Michael Cahill, *Francis Libermann's Commentary on the Gospel of St John. An investigation of the Rabbinical and French School*, Paraclete Press, Dublin, 1987, p 21. Cahill goes on to say that P. Sigrist, L. Cognet, J. Lecuyer and P. Blanchard agree that a change came about when he left Rennes. Ibid

4. Op. cit., chaps 2-44

5. *Qui était François Libermann?* In *Libermann (1802-1852)*, eds Coulon and Brasseur, Cerf, Paris 1998, p 66

generally, opened up a new perspective on the world in the late
1960s. Irish political life changed significantly; church life,
despite Vatican II, remained static for the most part. Questions
were put to church leaders and the responses were inadequate.
'We do not need to change, we are all right' was the general
attitude.

In the light of the gospel, the church is always called to
conversion. It was obvious that 'pagans' needed to be converted
but not 'Catholic Ireland'. The case being made here is that the
church in Ireland and in the 'developed' world needs more than
repair of cracks and leaks. A general reconstruction is needed
that has to begin with conversion.

This conversion is a gift, a grace from God that gives one a
new outlook and a changed attitude to life. St Paul's conversion
is a prototype of this. It is not a change from being irreligious to
being religious but of a very significant change in mind and in
behaviour. The crisis in the Catholic Church in Ireland and in
the Western world calls out for conversion within the church
structures. Vatican II was a start. It signalled a 'top/down'
reform but that is not enough. To be effective the movement has
to come from below also. Libermann realised that the church
was too centred on Rome and the local church ought to have
freedom while recognising the inter-dependence of the churches
that together constitute the Catholic Church. (p 79-85)

Where the media refer to the church, for instance, reference is
to bishops, priests and perhaps religious. If conversion failed at
that level then decline was inevitable. Young people began to
drift and a landslide followed. The opening to the world by
Pope John XXIII in his encyclicals *Mater et Magistra* and *Pacem in
Terris* on social issues and Vatican II in church affairs had little
effect. In the meantime a new culture was being formed.

The Holy Spirit

We have already referred to Libermann's criticism of a particular form of spiritual direction. He might well be passing
judgement then on a method that he had shared in the past with
Ferret but had abandoned by then. They appear to have had a
good relationship that broke down at this time. It is clear that in
1840 Libermann had become opposed to any rigid system of

spirituality being followed. Priority was to be given to the action
of the Holy Spirit. He writes with conviction in rejecting much
more forcefully than the remark of Ferret would seem to
warrant. He had come to recognise the action of the Spirit on the
seminarians he was advising and on his own life also. The Spirit
was seen to lead him and others in ways that seemed foolish and
imprudent in the estimation of the world.

In 1840 he wrote to Luquet:

> A guiding principle in divine affairs is not to draw everyone
> to one's own ideas and ways of behaving. Inflexibility in
> these matters produces deplorable results. God has a plan for
> each one; he gives his grace in different ways; and if we try to
> have our own way, we will never succeed in changing others.
> If at times in similar cases we have our way, it is others who
> suffer. Furthermore, one must not be assured of being right;
> but rather question oneself for fear of falling into a kind of
> interior inflexibility, which is very harmful. (ND. II, 124)

Four years after his conversion to mission he writes to a
friend who is troubled about making a decision and who is not
happy with his spiritual director:

> I don't know how you are being directed. Take it as a funda-
> mental principle that the one being directed is not to be harassed.
> He must not be given too many rules. In the spiritual life a
> system need not be adhered to strictly, in doing so people are
> damaged. If your director is pushing you too hard and is too
> insistent on principles with you he is perhaps acting wrongly.
> I see it as of great importance in direction to let grace work
> with true freedom. (ND. VI, 13)

This is what can be considered as a missionary outlook. The
person or community sets the agenda. The missionary does not
carry a set of rules with him. He does not come to a situation
with a system to be implemented. He comes to serve an
individual or community, to listen and enable people to attend
to their needs. Too often, centres of power in the church try to
control the Spirit that is not allowed to breathe freely over the
chaos in the world.

Structures

One can find in the outline of his missionary methodology we have been giving, a real concern for the poor and oppressed, a constant effort to be faithful to God and a willingness to be led by the Holy Spirit. An 'institutional' dimension needs to be considered also. It is great to have concern for a good cause. It is quite different to do something in the interest of the cause. Libermann had two basic issues in mind that were essential for getting involved in the mission. First, the mission had to be an integral part of the mission of the Catholic Church. Second, it would be operated by an approved religious society.

The basic structures that he had to establish were forming a religious community and getting approval from Rome. His first decision after his conversion was to go to Rome and present his project to the Pope. He began to write a provisional rule for community then. While he was firm with regard to the basic plan he was flexible as to details. The welfare of the oppressed was the overall guiding principle. The rule was provisional and could change according to changing conditions and growth in experience. His practice with Rome was to submit policies and proposals for consideration. (Lobbying was not excluded! Luquet did quite a bit.)

He kept in contact with the Roman authorities throughout his life while always remaining faithful to the missionary ideal he believed came from the Holy Spirit. He had very good relations with the church authorities and gained support from them for his projects. The structural elements were secondary and subordinated to the plan of God for the project. He knew that a missionary project would require some innovative factors and this could cause problems with Roman authorities, so careful diplomacy was required.

Although he deplored what he called 'the move towards centralisation' in church affairs (p 94) he still worked within the system as he found it and constantly provided input to the system that minimised the centralisation. He rarely spoke *about* Rome, but frequently *to* Rome. When minor officials in Rome tried to get him change his plans he stood firm and eventually succeeded in remaining faithful to his original vision. (p 43) Mission was God's mission; church and congregation were to serve and promote this. If Rome refused to recognise his proposal to form a missionary society he would have withdrawn from the project. He realised at an early stage that Le Vavasseur and Tisserant had in mind a very worthy cause but lacked the ability to carry it through.

Having got approval for the basic structure of the apostolate, more had to be done. For the mission work on the ground he proposed setting up a school system and a seminary to form an indigenous clergy. The schools and seminary would be adapted to the needs of the people. We have seen how his ideas for the seminary developed, for instance. He drew up an outline for the creation of dioceses and proposed the re-establishment of Minor Orders but these needed Roman approval which was refused.

In Ireland a number of people like Catherine McAuley and Ignatius Rice pioneered setting up schools to help the poor. Now the state has taken responsibility for providing education so new pioneers are needed to serve where needed. A new reality has to be faced now in education. New methods are required with proposals for different procedures.[6] Creativity is needed and some creative tensions could result. The pioneers in the past had their problems.

Libermann was aware of the inadequacy of the parish structure in ministering to the working class in the French cities. With the Industrial Revolution a new culture had emerged. The factory workers constituted a new class in society. For a ministry to these he was anxious 'to start a ministry that would embrace all the poorer classes ...' (p 91). The parish structure had become out-dated. A radical social change had taken place that required new religious thinking and new structures. Libermann had some knowledge of what Karl Marx was proposing and saw some merit in it. 'Communism is not to be feared ... ' (p 105). In most church teaching Marx was condemned.[7] Little enthusiasm

6. Some pioneering work has been done by Spiritans for their schools in setting up DEA.
7. Marx's description of religion as 'the opium of the people' seems to have been widely known. The context is less well known. 'Religious suffering is at one and the same time the expression of real suffering and a protest against real suffering. Religion is the sigh of the oppressed creature, the heart of a heartless world and the soul of soulless conditions. It is the opium of the people.'

for Trades Unions came from the clergy. The industrial workers left the church *en masse*. Or did the church abandon the working class? In pre-industrialised Ireland church attendance remained high, but as one observer remarked 'the full church was perhaps the opium of the clergy'.[8]

Secularism is among the '... isms' causing anxiety at present. Perhaps it need not be feared. It can be taken in a positive manner and our enemies can teach us if we are ready to listen. 'Protecting the faith' is frequently synonymous with 'controlling the institutions'.

Peace in time of turmoil
Libermann had seen church structures established in West Africa. Bishop Barron got a vast territory as a Vicariate. He did not have the resources nor the community support required for the work. He got discouraged and left. Libermann took up the challenge. He arranges to have a bishop appointed. Bishop Truffet proved to be totally unsuited as Vicar Apostolic. His idea of community was somewhat of the Cistercian model and self-denial was akin to starvation. He and most of the community were dead after six months in Africa. Libermann was traumatised; he realised that he bore some responsibility for the disaster but still continued with the mission even when it seemed impossible. He got two bishops, Bessieux and Kobes, appointed to the Vicariate and sent more priests.

The Irish church is in a crisis such that some observers see it as a terminal decay. The spotlight is on the bishops. They are seen to be the church and so their failures and incompetence are seen as the prognosis of immanent death. The Vatican also is not exempt from blame; and for many the pope in the Vatican is The Church *par excellence*! Can Libermann give any help in this situation?

His idea of the local church, later affirmed by Vatican II, can contribute to promoting the 'corporate responsibility' that now is been applied to the bishops and diocesan officials only. The laity have responsibilities too. Libermann's problem with 'centralisation' in the church, far from undermining the role of the papacy,

---

8. Michael Paul Gallagher SJ

protects that ministry and frees it from responsibilities it cannot
realistically take on itself. Then as a process of healing we look at a
letter to a young bishop who has succeeded another whose
imprudence caused his premature death and the deaths of his
fellow missionaries.

An extract from the last letter written by Libermann gives an
insight into the mind and heart of a missionary. It was written
on 1 November 1851 to Bishop Kobes in Dakar, Senegal, just
three months before he died when he was writing *Instructions*.

> Now more than ever I see that our lives should be lives of
> total sacrifice. We should come to such a degree of abandon-
> ment (*abnégation*) of ourselves in small matters and in great
> that we remain unperturbed by whatever happens to us. In
> the midst of all our pains and sufferings, in difficulties of
> every kind, we ought to stand before God in peace, humility,
> gentleness and with full confidence in the mercy of God.
> Nothing should elate us, nothing cause us to despair. We
> should control our joy in success and be patient in adversity.
> We should preserve serenity of spirit always as men totally
> dependent on God alone. We are doing God's work, in God
> and for God and he will fulfil his plans. Our joy ought to be
> gentle and peaceful whether we succeed or find we are
> stopped in our tracks. (ND, X111, 352)

'Sacrifice and self-denial' were very much part of Libermann's
religious vocabulary before his missionary apostolate. He emphasises their importance in his theological writings also. He often
quotes Mk 8:34: 'Whoever wishes to come after me, must deny
himself, take up his cross and follow me' to support his view. As
advice to a bishop thirty-one years old who is replacing another
who had died at the age of thirty-five after two hundred days in
Africa seems very imprudent and dangerous. These and similar
notions are very rare in his letters and when mentioned it is
usually to caution against excesses.[9] Perhaps he feared that the
ego of such a young man could be unduly inflated by the mitre.

In the crisis in the Irish church one would wish to find more of

---

9. Blanchard, Vol I, 423-444 has most references to his formal writings
and letters prior to 1841. He does not see the importance of the second
conversion.

the sense of dependence on God, on peace, humility, gentleness, serenity and moderation in the leadership. The failures of the past might help to bring about a more peaceful and spiritual ethos to the office of bishops in the country. Catholics are more disposed now to see bishops as weak and fallible human beings. The gospels portray the apostles as they were, 'warts and all'. The Christian, in whatever position, stands before God as a sinful and vulnerable human. Catholics have to face the judgements of the world with a sense of equanimity and face the judgement of God trusting in his merciful love.

To find missionaries portrayed as warriors and saints doesn't give a true picture but is quite a common one in missionary magazines. The majority of missionaries were not heroes. Many of them had little to show as a result of their ministry. Those who laid the foundations often seemed to labour in vain. Contemporary 'celebrity' culture has its dangers. To use the poor and the oppressed for one's own self-advancement doesn't correspond to the ethos of the New Testament. This is where *abnégation* applies. The well-resourced missionary could disable a poor community with generous donations. 'They bring money and goods, yes, they help but they do not love us' is a comment that is made about some missionaries by members of their churches. This hurts, of course, but could be therapeutic if taken on board. Not all missionary practices are to be recommended for home use. Libermann had to remind one very zealous missionary that 'kicking his people was not very evangelical'.

'Jesus sent out the twelve after instructing them thus, "Do not go into pagan territory or enter a Samaritan town. Go rather to the lost sheep of the house of Israel".' (Mt 10:5-6) 'Go and make disciples of all nations.' (Mt 28:19) The mission of the church is exercised at home and abroad. A good deal can be learned from 'our fathers in the faith'. Libermann has much to teach us in relation to the church's mission today. Ultimately, however, it is to Jesus we must go for direction and inspiration in mission apostolate. Jesus' triumphal entry into Jerusalem is in no way a measure of his success. The events of Good Friday do not prove that his ministry failed.

In 1850 Libermann was very severely criticised by Le Vavasseur in a letter with a vitriolic attack on Libermann's leadership and the policies of the congregation. The most hostile media critic of the leadership in the Irish church would scarcely be so scathing. Libermann replied in a gentle but firm manner. Just to take one example:

> You say we are incapable of managing the seminary. But neither are we able to manage the congregation, but at the beginning we were infinitely less capable. If we do not have to depend on God we might as well take off immediately to the desert and not get involved in God's affairs. Who then would do God's work? The learned? The experts? With that kind of reasoning nobody genuinely religious would take on an important function because such persons would feel they were not able for it. This would result in leaving to those who have a high opinion of themselves the important functions and those are the very ones incapable of carrying out God's plan. No, you are not in God's truth. Poor though we are, we will succeed if we remain faithful. We must not be driven by our own minds, by our own presumptions in God's affairs. If, however, God is directing us, woe to us if we pull out! We have to trust in God and he will not let us down. (ND, XII, 200)

Such a letter shows Libermann's respect for his missionaries. If they were to work for the poor they needed all the support he could give. To encourage his men at the coalface was a major part of Libermann's mission. When he himself was under attack it was not his ego that had to be saved but the missionaries and their mission. Priests and religious Brothers and Sisters have been under attack in Ireland and with reason. Who gives the support and encouragement that they need? They have few friends now. One wonders is this because of the damage done to children or to the church. The media will see to the blame and the criticism will be harsh. Le Vavasseur wasn't very gentle in his criticism. He was demanding perfection in personnel and in administration. In his reply, Libermann even added a PS to his letter:

> Despite the harsh things you have said in your letter, you have done me a great favour. It has given me new commitment to use all in my power to serve God and the poor countries. My

hope is greater than ever precisely because the situation seems so hopeless. (ND. XII, 204}

Church leadership seems unable to cope with mistakes and harsh criticism that should be seen as a stimulus to change and to hope. From a position of prestige and considerable achievements it is difficult to face harsh or even fair criticism. Libermann's spirituality was grounded on the gospels and the letters of Paul. In his theological writings he tends to quote from the New Testament in support of his position. His letters, on the other hand, rarely use quotations but express the truths of scripture in conventional letter-writing genre. The excerpt given above is an illustration of 1 Cor 1:20-30: 'God chose the foolish of the world to shame the wise.' He is not at all apologetic for the weakness of the missionaries and his own role in leadership. He appears quite sure that God's plan will succeed because the mission was God's mission. He with his fellow missionaries had to give of their best. Their resources are so weak they had to rely on God. While their faith was firm then success was assured. They were followers of the Crucified One.